Afghan ENCHANTMENT™

the Needlecraft™ Shop

Afghan ENCHANTMENT™

Publisher: Donna Robertson
Design Director: Fran Rohus
Production Director: Ange Workman

Editorial
Senior Editor: Jennifer Christiansen Simcik
Editor: Sharon Lothrop
Associate Editors: Jana Robertson, Trudy Atteberry
Graphics Assistant: Kristine Kirst
Copy Editors: Marianne Telesca, Kim Pierce

Photography
Photographers: Mary Craft,
Tammy Cromer-Campbell
Photo Stylist/Coordinator: Ruth Whitaker
Cover Photograph: Tammy Cromer-Campbell

Book Design/Production
Production Manager: Glenda Chamberlain

Product Design
Brenda Wendling, Design Coordinator

Business
John Robinson, CEO
Karen Pierce, Vice President/Customer Service
Greg Deily, Vice President/Marketing
John Trotter, Vice President/M.I.S.

Credits
Sincerest thanks to all the designers, manufacturers
and other professionals whose dedication has
made this book possible. Special thanks to
David Norris and Kaye Stafford of
Quebecor Printing Book Group, Kingsport, TN.
Copyright © 1996 The Needlecraft Shop, LLC
All rights reserved. No part of this book may be
reproduced in any form or by any means without the written
permission of the publisher, excepting brief quotations in
connection with reviews written specifically for inclusion in
magazines, newspapers and other publications.

Library of Congress Cataloging-in-Publication Data
ISBN: 1-57367-036-7
First Printing: 1995
Library of Congress Catalog Card Number: 95-69227
Published and Distributed by
The Needlecraft Shop, LLC, Big Sandy, Texas 75755
Printed in the United States of America.

Cover: *Love in Bloom*, pattern begins on page 81.

*D*ear Friends —

Imagine the scene. You're standing at the entrance to a lush, tranquil garden, filled with a symphony of radiant blossoms and verdant greenery. As you survey its calming serenity, you find yourself irresistibly drawn to its exquisite beauty. Now, translate that feeling to a different Eden, a magical kingdom bursting forth with an unparalleled array of exclusive afghan designs found nowhere else. This beautiful book is your key, and with it, I'd like to issue an invitation to you to enter this fascinating wonderland.

As you journey through this romantic paradise, you'll find an artful blend of old and new, traditional and modern, all in a captivating collection that will inspire and delight for years to come. Each remarkable chapter is filled with a stunning assortment of graceful creations suitable for every decor, every desire.

We hope you enjoy your visit to this fantastic place, an adventure you can take each time you open this book. Our utmost care went into the production of this distinctive volume, with every aspect carefully considered for your total crochet pleasure.

Bon Voyage!

Jennifer

Contents

Transport yourself back to an innocent
age of sophisticated grace when elegance
was an everyday pleasure. This spirited
collection lets you capture the romance
and magic of days gone by in a medley
of touchable old-fashioned designs
with up-to-date charm. Your home will
take on a character all its own accented
with these expressive beauties in a
wonderous array of colors and styles.

Captivating Nostalgia

BY KATHERINE ENG

Remembrance Rose

Finished Size: 46" x 65½"

Materials: Worsted-weight yarn — 19 oz. off-white, 17½ oz. rose and 16½ oz. pink; tapestry needle; G crochet hook or size needed to obtain gauge.

Gauge: 4 sc sts = 1"; 4 sc rows = 1". Each Block is 6½" square.

Skill Level: ✦✦ Average

SQUARE (make 54)

Rnd 1: With pink, ch 5, sl st in first ch to form ring, ch 1, 16 sc in ring, join with sl st in first sc (16 sc).

Notes: For **beginning cluster (beg cl),** ch 4, *yo 2 times, insert hook in same st, yo, draw lp through, (yo, draw through 2 lps on hook) 2 times; repeat from * 2 more times, yo, draw through all 4 lps on hook.

For **cluster (cl),** yo 2 times, insert hook in next st, yo, draw lp through, (yo, draw through 2 lps on hook) 2 times, *yo 2 times, insert hook in same st, yo, draw lp through, (yo, draw through 2 lps on hook) 2 times; repeat from * 2 more times, yo, draw through all 5 lps on hook.

Rnd 2: Beg cl, ch 5, skip next st, sc in next st, ch 5, skip next st, (cl in next st, ch 5, skip next st, sc in next st, ch 5) around, join with sl st in top of first cl, fasten off (4 cl, 4 sc).

Rnd 3: Join off-white with sc in ch-5 sp before any cl, sc in same sp, ch 1, 2 sc in next ch-5 sp, ch 4, sc in next sc, ch 4, (2 sc in next ch-5 sp, ch 1, 2 sc in next ch-5 sp, ch 4, sc in next sc, ch 4) around, join with sl st in first sc (20 sc, 8 ch-4 sps, 4 ch-1 sps).

Rnd 4: Ch 1, sc in first st, *[hdc in next st, (2 dc, ch 2, 2 dc) in next ch-1 sp, hdc in next st, sc in next st, sc in next ch-4 sp, ch 3, sc in next ch-4 sp], sc in next sc; repeat from * 2 more times; repeat between [ ], join.

Rnd 5: Ch 1, sc in first st, *[ch 1, skip next st, sc in next st, ch 1, skip next st, (sc, ch 2, sc) in next corner ch sp, (ch 1, skip next st, sc in next st) 2 times, ch 1, skip next st, (sc, ch 1, sc) in next ch-3 sp, ch 1, skip next st], sc in next st; repeat from * 2 more times; repeat between [ ], join, fasten off.

Rnd 6: Join pink with sc in any corner ch-2 sp, ch 3, sc in same sp, ch 3, (sc, ch 3) in each ch sp around with (sc, ch 3, sc, ch 3) in each corner ch sp, join, fasten off.

Rnd 7: Working in sc on row before last behind ch sps on last row, join rose with sc in st before any corner; *for **corner,** ch 4; sc in next sc, (ch 1, sc in next sc) 7 times; repeat from * 2 more times, ch 4, (sc in next sc, ch 1) 7 times, join.

Rnd 8: Ch 1, sc in each st and in each ch-1 sp around with (2 sc, ch 2, 2 sc) in each corner ch-4 sp, join, **turn** (19 sc in each side between corner ch sps).

Rnd 9: Sl st in next st, ch 1, sc in same st, *ch 1, skip next st, (sc in next st, ch 1, skip next st) across to next corner, (sc, ch 2, sc) in next corner ch sp; repeat from * 3 more times, ch 1, skip next st, sc in next st, ch 1, skip next st, join, **turn,** fasten off.

Rnd 10: Join off-white with sc in any corner ch sp, ch 3, sc in same sp, *[(sc, ch 1) in each sc across to one st before next corner, sc in next st], (sc, ch 3, sc) in next corner ch sp; repeat from * 2 more times; repeat between [ ], join, fasten off (23 sts and ch-1 sps on each

Continued on page 22

Falling Leaves

Finished Size: 48" x 74"

Materials: Worsted-weight yarn — 40 oz. tan, 8½ oz. brown and 5 oz. rust; G crochet hook or size needed to obtain gauge.

Gauge: 4 dc sts = 1"; 2 dc rows = 1".

Skill Level: ✧✧ Average

PANEL (make 5)

Notes: For **block,** dc in each of next 3 sts, or, 2 dc in next ch sp, dc in next st.

For **mesh,** ch 2, skip next 2 chs or sts, dc in next st.

Row 1: With tan, ch 30, dc in 4th ch from hook, dc in each ch across, turn (28 dc). Front of row 1 is right side of work.

Row 2: For row 2 of graph, ch 3, block, mesh 2 times, block 3 times, mesh 2 times, block, turn.

Rows 3-23: Ch 3, work according to graph across, turn.

Rows 24-131: Repeat rows 2-23 consecutively, ending with row 21.

Rnd 132: For **first, third and fifth Panels,** with right side facing you, working around outer edge in sts and in ends of rows, join brown with sc in first st on last row, ch 3, sc in same st, *(ch 2, skip next 2 sts, sc in next st) 2 times, (ch 2, skip next st, sc in next st) 3 times, ch 2, skip next 2 sts, sc in next st, (ch 2, skip next st, sc in next st) 3 times, (ch 2, skip next 2 sts, sc in next st) 2 times, ch 3, sc in same st as last st, ch 2, skip first row, sc in next row (ch 2, sc in next row) across*; working on opposite side of starting ch, (sc, ch 3, sc) in first st; repeat between **, join with sl st in first sc, fasten off (11 ch-2 sps on each short end between corner ch-3 sps, 131 ch-2 sps on each long edge between corner ch-3 sps).

Rnd 132: For **second and fourth Panels,**
with wrong side facing you and reversing Panels according to Assembly Diagram on page 23, repeat rnd 132 for first, third and fifth Panels.

Rnd 133: Join rust with sc in first ch sp, ch 3, sc in same sp, ch 2, (sc, ch 2) in each ch-2 sp around with (sc, ch 3, sc, ch 2) in each corner ch-3 sp, join, fasten off.

Rnd 134: With brown, repeat rnd 133.

Rnd 135: For **first Panel** only, with tan, repeat rnd 133.

Rnd 135: For **remaining Panels,** join tan with sc in top right-hand corner ch sp (see diagram), ch 3, sc in same sp, ch 2, (sc in next ch sp, ch 2) across to next corner ch sp, *sc in next corner sp, ch 2, drop lp from hook, insert hook from back to front through corresponding corner ch-3 sp on last Panel, draw dropped lp through, ch 2, sc in same sp on this Panel as last sc*, (ch 1, drop lp from hook, insert hook from back to front through next ch-2 sp on last Panel, draw dropped lp through, ch 1, sc in next ch-2 sp on this Panel) across to next corner ch sp, ch 2; repeat between **, ch 2, (sc, ch 2) in each ch-2 sp around with (sc, ch 3, sc, ch 2) in last corner ch-3 sp, join with sl st in first sc, fasten off.

BORDER

Rnd 1: Join tan with sc in top right-hand corner ch sp, ch 3, sc in same sp, ch 2, (sc, ch 2) in each ch-2 sp and in each ch-3 sp on each

Continued on page 23

Vintage Grapes

Finished Size: 55" x 66"

Materials: Worsted-weight yarn — 30 oz. off-white,
20 oz. purple and 14 oz. green;
I crochet hook or size needed to obtain gauge.

Gauge: Rnd 1 = 2½" across; 3 shell rnds = 2½".
Each Block is 11" square.

Skill Level: ✦✦ Average

FIRST ROW
First Block
Notes: For **beginning popcorn (beg pc),** ch 4, 4 tr in same sp or ring, drop lp from hook, insert hook in top of ch-4, pick up dropped lp, draw through ch.

For **popcorn (pc),** 5 tr in next ch sp or ring, drop lp from hook, insert hook in first st of 5-dc group, pick up dropped lp, draw through st.

Rnd 1: With purple, ch 6, sl st in first ch to form ring, beg pc, ch 4, (pc, ch 4) 5 times, join with sl st in top of first pc (6 pc, 6 ch-4 sps).

Rnd 2: Sl st in first ch sp, (beg pc, ch 4, pc, ch 4) in same sp, (pc, ch 4) 2 times in each ch-4 sp around, join, fasten off (12 pc, 12 ch sps).

Rnd 3: Join green with sl st in any ch sp, (ch 4, tr, ch 3, 2 tr) in same sp, (2 tr, ch 3, 2 tr) in each ch sp around, join with sl st in top of ch-4, fasten off.

Note: For **shell,** (3 dc, ch 2, 3 dc) in next ch sp.

Rnd 4: Join off-white with sl st in any ch sp, (beg pc, ch 4, pc) in same sp, ch 4, shell in next ch sp, ch 2, shell in next ch sp, ch 4, *(pc, ch 4, pc) in next ch sp, ch 4, shell in next ch sp, ch 2, shell in next ch sp, ch 4; repeat from * around, join with sl st in first pc.

Rnd 5: Sl st in next ch-4 sp, (beg pc, ch 4, pc, ch 4, pc) in same sp, ch 4, shell in ch sp of next shell, ch 2, shell in ch sp of next shell, ch 4, *(pc, ch 4) 3 times in next ch sp, shell in ch sp of next shell, ch 2, shell in ch sp of next

shell, ch 4; repeat from * around, join.

Rnd 6: Sl st in next ch sp, (beg pc, ch 4, pc) in same sp, ch 5, (pc, ch 4, pc) in next ch sp, ch 4, shell in next shell, ch 2, shell in next shell, ch 4, *(pc, ch 4, pc) in next ch sp, ch 5, (pc, ch 4, pc) in next ch sp, ch 4, shell in next shell, ch 2, shell in next shell, ch 4; repeat from * around, join, fasten off.

Second Block
Rnds 1-5: Repeat same rnds of First Block.

Notes: For **corner joining,** ch 2, drop lp from hook, insert hook from front to back through corresponding ch-5 sp on other Block, pull dropped lp through, ch 3.

For **side joining,** ch 2, drop lp from hook, insert hook from front to back through next ch-4 sp on other Block, pull dropped lp through, ch 2.

For **joined shell,** 3 dc in next shell on this Block, ch 1, drop lp from hook, pull through ch sp of next shell on other Block, ch 1, 3 dc in same shell on this Block.

Rnd 6: Sl st in next ch sp, (beg pc, ch 4, pc) in same sp; working on side of last Block, work corner joining (see Joining Diagram on page 24), pc in next ch sp on this Block, work side joining, pc in same ch sp on this Block, work side joining, work joined shell, ch 2, worked joined shell, work side joining, pc in next ch sp on this Block, work side joining, pc in same ch

Continued on page 24

Sentimental Journey

Finished Size: 45" x 65"

Materials: Chunky mohair-like yarn — 22 oz. lavender, 16 oz. dk. green, 4½ oz. green/purple variegated; chunky yarn — 9 oz. purple; tapestry needle; G crochet hook or size needed to obtain gauge.

Gauge: 4 sts = 1". Rows 1-6 of Panel = 2¾".

Skill Level: ✧✧ Average

PANEL (make 7)

Row 1: With lavender, ch 210, sc in 2nd ch from hook, sc in each of next 2 chs, *[hdc in each of next 2 chs, dc in each of next 2 chs, tr in next ch, (tr, ch 2, tr) in next ch, tr in next ch, dc in each of next 2 chs, hdc in each of next 2 chs], sc in next 5 chs; repeat from * 11 more times; repeat between [ ], sc in each of last 3 chs, turn, fasten off (222 sts).

Row 2: Join green with sl st in first st, ch 1, sc first 2 sts tog, (ch 1, skip next st, sc in next st) 3 times, ch 1, skip next st, *(sc, ch 2, sc) in next ch sp, (ch 1, skip next st, sc in next st) 4 times, skip next st, (sc in next st, ch 1, skip next st) 4 times; repeat from * 11 more times, (sc, ch 2, sc) in next ch sp, (ch 1, skip next st, sc in next st) 3 times, ch 1, skip next st, sc last 2 sts tog, turn, fasten off (104 ch-1 sps, 12 ch-2 sps).

Row 3: Join purple with sl st in first ch-1 sp, ch 4, (dc in next ch-1 sp, ch 1) 3 times, *[(dc, ch 2, dc) in next ch-2 sp, (ch 1, dc in next ch-1 sp) 4 times], skip next 2 sc, (dc in next ch sp, ch 1) 4 times; repeat from * 11 more times; repeat between [ ], turn, fasten off.

Row 4: Join variegated with sc in first ch sp, (ch 1, sc in next ch sp) 3 times, ch 1, *[(sc, ch 2, sc) in next ch-2 sp, (ch 1, sc in next ch sp) 4 times], ch 1, skip next 2 dc, (sc in next ch sp, ch 1) 4 times; repeat from * 11 more times; repeat between [ ], turn, fasten off.

Row 5: Join lavender with sl st in first ch sp, ch 4, tr in same sp, (ch 1, dc in next ch sp) 2 times, ch 1, hdc in next ch sp, ch 1, *[sl st in next ch-2 sp, ch 1, hdc in next ch sp, (ch 1, dc in next ch sp) 2 times, ch 1], skip next ch-1 sp, 5 tr in next ch sp, ch 1, skip next ch-1 sp, (dc in next ch sp, ch 1) 2 times, hdc in next ch sp, ch 1; repeat from * 11 more times; repeat between [ ], 2 tr in last ch sp, turn.

Row 6: Working in sts and in ch sps, ch 1, sc in first st, (ch 1, skip next st or ch sp, sc in next st or ch sp) across, turn, fasten off (130 sc).

Row 7: With right side of row 1 facing you, working in starting ch on opposite side of row 1, join lavender with sc in first ch, sc in each of next 2 chs, *[hdc in each of next 2 chs, dc in each of next 2 chs, tr in next ch, (tr, ch 2, tr) in next ch, tr in next ch, dc in each of next 2 chs, hdc in each of next 2 chs], sc in next 5 chs; repeat from * 11 more times; repeat between [ ], sc in each of last 3 chs, turn, fasten off (222 sts).

Rows 8-12: Repeat rows 2-6.

Holding Panels right sides together, matching sts, with lavender, sew long edges together through **back lps**.

BORDER

Rnd 1: With right side facing you, working in ends of rows across one short end, join lavender with sc in first row, *ch 2, sc in same row, evenly space 22 more sc across Panel to

Continued on page 25

BY KATHERINE ENG

Terrace Dreams

Finished Size: 42" x 62"

Materials: Worsted-weight yarn — 14 oz. med. mint, 13 oz. lt. mint, 12 oz. lt. lavender and 11 oz. med. lavender; G crochet hook or size needed to obtain gauge.

Gauge: 4 sc sts = 1"; 4 sc rows = 1".

Skill Level: ✧✧ Average

AFGHAN

Row 1: With lt. lavender, ch 208, sc in 2nd ch from hook, sc in next 7 chs, (sc, ch 2, sc) in next ch, *sc in next 8 chs, skip next 2 chs, sc in next 8 chs, (sc, ch 2, sc) in next ch, repeat from * across to last 8 chs, sc in last 8 chs, turn (198 sc).

Row 2: Ch 1, sc first 2 sts tog, *[(ch 1, skip next st, sc in next st) 3 times, ch 1, skip next st, (sc, ch 2, sc) in next ch-2 sp], (ch 1, skip next st, sc in next st) 4 times, skip next 2 sts, sc in next st; repeat from * 9 more times; repeat between [ ], (ch 1, skip next st, sc in next st) 3 times, ch 1, skip next st, sc last 2 sts tog, turn, fasten off.

Row 3: Join lt. mint with sl st in first st, ch 1, sc first st and next ch sp tog, sc in next 7 sts and ch sps, *(sc, ch 2, sc) in next ch-2 sp, sc in next 8 sts and ch sps, skip next 2 sts, sc in next 8 sts and ch sps; repeat from * 9 more times, (sc, ch 2, sc) in next ch-2 sp, sc in next 7 sts and ch sps, sc last ch sp and st tog, turn.

Row 4: Repeat row 2.

Row 5: Join med. lavender with sl st in first st, ch 1, sc first 2 sts tog, *[(ch 4, sc in next ch-1 sp) 3 times, ch 4, (sc, ch 4, sc) in next ch-2 sp], (ch 4, sc in next ch-1 sp) 4 times, skip next 2 sts, sc in next ch sp; repeat from * 9 more times; repeat between [ ], (ch 4, sc in next ch sp) 3 times, ch 4, sc last ch sp and st tog, **do not turn**, fasten off.

Row 6: Working in worked ch sps on row before last behind ch sps on last row, join lt. mint with sc in first ch-1 sp, *[(ch 1, sc in next ch-1 sp working on left-hand side of med. lavender st) 3 times, ch 1, sc in next ch-2 sp working on right-hand side of med. lavender sts, ch 2, sc in same ch-2 sp on left-hand side of med. lavender sts, (ch 1, sc in next ch-1 sp working on right-hand side of med. lavender st) 4 times], skip next 2 sts, sc in next ch-1 sp on left-hand side of med. lavender st; repeat from * 9 more times; repeat between [ ], turn.

Row 7: Ch 1, sc first st and next ch sp tog, *[(ch 1, sc in next ch sp) 3 times, ch 1, (sc, ch 2, sc) in next ch-2 sp], (ch 1, sc in next ch-1 sp) 4 times, skip next 2 sts, sc in next ch sp; repeat from * 9 more times; repeat between [ ], (ch 1, sc in next ch-1 sp) 3 times, ch 1, sc last ch sp and st tog, turn, fasten off.

Rows 8-9: With lt. lavender, repeat rows 3 and 2.

Rows 10-11: With med. mint, repeat rows 3 and 2.

Row 12: Repeat row 5.

Rows 13-14: With med. mint, repeat rows 6 and 7.

Rows 15-16: Repeat rows 8 and 9.

Rows 17-178: Repeat rows 3-16 consecutively, ending with row 10. At end of last row, fasten off.

Row 179: Working in starting ch on opposite side of row 1, join med. mint with sc in

Continued on page 25

Picnic in the Park

Finished Size: 53½" x 64"

Materials: Worsted-weight yarn — 18 oz. brown, 12 oz. blue, 10 oz. each green and tan, and 6 oz. burgundy; H crochet hook or size needed to obtain gauge.

Gauge: 7 dc sts = 2"; 5 dc rows = 3". Each Block is 10½" square.

Skill Level: ✧✧ Average

BLOCK (make 30)

Rnd 1: With burgundy, ch 4, sl st in first ch to form ring, ch 3, 3 dc in ring, ch 2, (4 dc in ring, ch 2) 3 times, join with sl st top of ch-3 (16 dc, 4 ch-2 sps).

Note: For **shell,** (2 dc, ch 2, 2 dc) in next ch sp.

Rnd 2: Ch 3, dc in each st around with shell in each corner ch sp, join, fasten off.

Rnd 3: Join green with sl st in 5th st after any corner ch sp, ch 3, dc in each of next 3 sts, *shell in next ch sp, dc in next 8 sts, shell in next ch sp*, dc in next 4 sts changing to tan (*see fig. 10, page 158*) in last st made, dc in next 4 sts; repeat between **, dc in last 4 sts, join, **turn.**

Rnd 4: Ch 3, (dc in next 6 sts, shell in next ch sp, dc in next 12 sts, shell in next ch sp), dc in next 6 sts changing to green in last st made; repeat between ( ), dc in last 5 sts, join, **turn.**

Rnd 5: Ch 3, dc in next 7 sts, (shell in next ch sp, dc in next 16 sts, shell in next ch sp), dc in next 8 sts changing to tan in last st made, dc in next 8 sts; repeat between ( ), dc in last 8 sts, join, **do not** turn, fasten off (20 sts on each side between corner ch sps).

Rnd 6: Working on the solid green side of rnd 5, join blue with sc in 11th st, ch 3, dc in next 9 sts, (shell in next ch sp, dc in next 20 sts, shell in next ch sp), dc in next 10 sts changing to brown in last st made, dc in next 10 sts; repeat between ( ), dc in last 10 sts, join, **turn.**

Rnd 7: Ch 3, (dc in next 12 sts, shell in next ch sp, dc in next 24 sts, shell in next ch sp), dc in next 12 sts changing to blue in last st made; repeat between ( ), dc in last 11 sts, join, **turn.**

Rnd 8: Ch 3, dc in next 13 sts, (shell in next ch sp, dc in next 28 sts, shell in next ch sp), dc in next 14 sts changing to brown in last st made, dc in next 14 sts; repeat between ( ), dc in last 14 sts, join, fasten off.

To **join** one side of Block, holding Blocks right sides together, matching sts; working through **front lps** only, join matching color with sc in first st, sc in each st across changing colors as needed to match Block, fasten off.

For **first strip,** hold one Block with blue at top and brown at bottom, join four more Blocks matching brown to brown and blue to blue. Repeat for five more strips.

Join strips together in same manner.

EDGING

Rnd 1: Join brown with sl st in any corner ch sp, (ch 3, 2 dc, ch 2, 3 dc) in same sp, [◊ch 2, skip next 2 sts, *(sc in next st, ch 2, skip next st) across to next joining, ch 2, sc in next ch sp before joining, ch 2, sc in next joining, ch 2*; repeat between ** across to next corner Block, (sc in next st, ch 2, skip next st) across◊, (3 dc, ch 2, 3 dc) in next corner ch sp]; repeat between [ ] 2 more times; repeat between ◊◊, join with sl st in top of ch-3.

Rnd 2: Sl st in each of next 2 sts, (sl st, ch 3, 2 dc, ch 2, 3 dc) in next ch sp, ch 2, (sc, ch 2) in each ch-2 sp around with (3 dc, ch 2, 3 dc, ch 2) in each corner ch sp, join, fasten off.

Remembrance Rose

Continued from page 10

edge between corner ch sps).

Holding Blocks wrong sides together, matching sts, sew together through **back lps** in six rows of nine Blocks each.

BORDER

Rnd 1: With right side facing you, join off-white with sc in any corner ch sp, ch 3, sc in same sp, sc in each st, sc in each ch-1 sp, sc in each ch sp on each side of seams and hdc in each seam around with (sc, ch 3, sc) in each corner ch sp, join with sl st first sc, **turn** (155 sts on each short end between corner ch sps, 233 sts on each long edge between corner ch sps).

Rnd 2: Sl st in next st, ch 1, sc in same st, *ch 1, skip next st, (sc in next st, ch 1, skip next st) across to next corner, (sc, ch 3, sc) in next corner ch sp; repeat from * 3 more times, ch 1, skip next st, join, **turn,** fasten off.

Rnd 3: Join rose with sc in first corner ch sp, ch 3, sc in same sp, *ch 1, (sc in next ch sp, ch 1) across to next corner, (sc, ch 3, sc) in next corner ch sp; repeat from * 2 more times, ch 1, (sc in next ch sp, ch 1) across, join.

Rnd 4: Sl st in next ch sp, (ch 3, dc, ch 2, 2 dc) in same sp, dc in each st and in each ch sp around with (2 dc, ch 2, 2 dc) in each corner ch sp, join with sl st in top of ch-3, **turn** (163 dc on each short end between corner ch sps, 241 dc on each long edge between corner ch sps).

Rnd 5: Ch 1, sc in first st, *ch 1, skip next st, (sc in next st, ch 1, skip next st) across to next corner, (sc, ch 3, sc) in next corner ch sp; repeat from * 3 more times, ch 1, skip next st, join with sl st in first sc, **turn,** fasten off.

Rnd 6: Join pink with sc in any corner ch sp, ch 3, sc in same sp, sc in each ch-1 sp and in each st around with (sc, ch 3, sc) in each corner ch sp, join (167 sc on each short end between corner ch sps, 245 sc on each long edge between corner ch sps).

Note: For **shell,** (2 dc, ch 2, 2 dc) in next st.

Rnd 7: (Sl st, ch 3, 2 dc, ch 3, 3 dc) in next ch sp, *[skip next 2 sts, sc in next st, skip next 2 sts, (shell in next st, skip next 2 sts, sc in next st, skip next 2 sts) across to next corner], (3 dc, ch 3, 3 dc) in next corner ch sp; repeat from * 2 more times; repeat between [ ], join with sl st in top of ch-3.

Rnd 8: (Sl st, ch 3, 2 dc, ch 2, 3 dc) in next st, ch 1, [◊(sc, ch 3, sc) in next corner ch sp, ch 1, skip next st, (3 dc, ch 2, 3 dc, ch 1) in next st, *(3 dc, ch 2, 3 dc, ch 1) in ch sp of each shell across to next corner, skip next sc and next dc◊, (3 dc, ch 2, 3 dc, ch 1) in next st]; repeat between [ ] 2 more times; repeat between ◊◊, join.

Rnd 9: Sl st in each of next 2 sts, (sl st, ch 1, sc, ch 3, sc) in next ch-2 sp, ch 3, sc in next ch-1 sp, [◊(sc, ch 3, sc, ch 5, sc, ch 3, sc) in next corner ch sp, sc in next ch-1 sp◊, *ch 3, (sc, ch 3, sc) in next ch-2 sp, ch 3, sc in next ch-1 sp*; repeat between ** across to next corner]; repeat between [ ] 3 more times, ch 3, join with sl st in first sc, fasten off.🔖

Falling Leaves

Continued from page 13

side of seams around with (sc, ch 3, sc, ch 2) in each corner ch-3 sp, join with sl st in first sc, fasten off (79 ch-2 sps on each short end between corner ch-3 sps, 135 ch-2 sps on each long edge between corner ch-3 sps).

Rnds 2-4: Following color sequence of brown, rust, brown, repeat rnd 133 of Panel.

Note: For **shell**, (2 dc, ch 2, 2 dc) in next st.

Rnd 5: Join tan with sl st in any corner ch sp, (ch 3, 2 dc, ch 3, 3 dc) in same ch sp, *[skip next st, sc in next st, (shell in next st, sc in next st) across to one st before next corner ch sp], (3 dc, ch 3, 3 dc) in next corner ch sp; repeat from * 2 more times; repeat between [ ], join with sl st in top of ch-3.

Rnd 6: Sl st in next st, ch 1, (sc, ch 3, sc) in same st, ch 1, [◊(sc, ch 3, sc, ch 4, sc, ch 3, sc) in next corner ch sp, ch 1, skip next dc, (sc, ch 3, sc) in next dc, ch 1, sc in next sc, *ch 1, (sc, ch 3, sc) in ch sp of next shell, ch 1, sc in next sc; repeat from * across to next corner, ch 1◊, skip next dc, (sc, ch 3, sc) in next dc, ch 1]; repeat between [ ] 2 more times; repeat between ◊◊, join with sl st in first sc, fasten off.✍

ASSEMBLY DIAGRAM

◆ = top right-hand corner

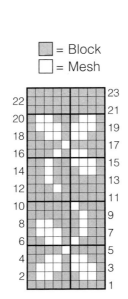

☐ = Block
☐ = Mesh

First Panel   Second Panel   Third Panel   Fourth Panel   Fifth Panel

Vintage Grapes

Continued from page 14

sp on this block, work corner joining, *[(pc, ch 4, pc) in next ch sp on this Block, ch 4, shell in next shell, ch 2, shell in next shell, ch 4], (pc, ch 4, pc) in next ch sp, ch 5; repeat from *; repeat between [ ], join, fasten off.

Repeat Second Block 3 more times for a total of 5 Blocks.

SECOND ROW
First Block

Joining to bottom of First Block on last row, work same as First Row Second Block.

Second Block

Rnds 1-5: Repeat same rnds of First Block.

Rnd 6: Sl st in next ch sp, (beg pc, ch 4, pc) in same sp; working on bottom of next Block on last row, work corner joining, *pc in next ch sp on this Block, work side joining, pc in same ch sp on this Block, work side joining, work joined shell, ch 2, work joined shell, work side joining, pc in next ch sp on this Block, work side joining, pc in same ch sp on this block, work corner joining*; working on

side of last Block on this row; repeat between **, [(pc, ch 4, pc) in next ch sp on this Block, ch 4, shell in next shell, ch 2, shell in next shell, ch 4]; repeat between [ ], join, fasten off.

Repeat Second Block 3 more times.

Repeat Second Row 4 more times for a total of 6 rows.

EDGING

Join off-white, with sl st in ch-5 sp before one short end, ch 3, 5 dc in same sp, ◊*[(sc in next pc, 6 dc in next ch sp) 2 times, sc in next dc, 6 dc in next ch sp, sc in next ch-2 sp, 6 dc in next ch sp, skip next 2 dc, sc in next dc, (6 dc in next ch sp, sc in next pc) 2 times, 6 dc in next ch-5 sp], sc in next joining, 6 dc in next ch-5 sp*; repeat between ** across to next corner Block; repeat between [ ]; repeat from ◊ 2 more times; repeat between ** across to next corner block, (sc in next pc, 6 dc in next ch sp) 2 times, sc in next dc, 6 dc in next ch sp, sc in next ch-2 sp, 6 dc in next ch sp, skip next 2 dc, sc in next dc, (6 dc in next ch sp, sc in next pc) 2 times, join with sl st in top of first ch-3, fasten off.🍂

JOINING DIAGRAM

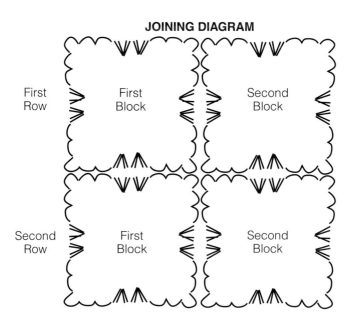

Sentimental Journey

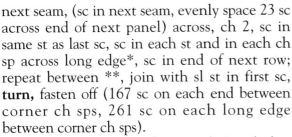

Continued from page 16

next seam, (sc in next seam, evenly space 23 sc across end of next panel) across, ch 2, sc in same st as last sc, sc in each st and in each ch sp across long edge*, sc in end of next row; repeat between **, join with sl st in first sc, **turn,** fasten off (167 sc on each end between corner ch sps, 261 sc on each long edge between corner ch sps).

Rnd 2: Join green with sc in ch-2 sp before one short end, ch 2, sc in same sp *[ch 1, skip next st, (sc in next st, ch 1, skip next st) across to next corner], (sc, ch 2, sc) in next corner ch sp; repeat from * 2 more times; repeat between [ ], join, **turn.**

Rnd 3: Sl st in next ch sp, ch 4, (dc, ch 1) in each ch-1 sp around with (2 dc, ch 2, 2 dc, ch 1) in each corner ch sp, join with sl st in 3rd ch of ch-4, **do not** turn.

Note: For **shell,** (3 dc, ch 3, 3 dc) in next ch sp.

Rnd 4: Sl st in next ch sp, sl st in next st, (sl st, ch 3, 2 dc, ch 3, 3 dc) in next ch sp, *(skip next 2 ch sps, sc in next ch sp, skip next ch sp, shell in next ch sp) across to 3 ch sps before next corner, skip next 2 ch sps, sc in next ch sp, shell in next corner ch sp, sc in next ch sp, skip next ch sp, (shell in next ch sp, skip next 2 ch sps, sc in next ch sp, skip next ch sp) across to 3 ch sps before next corner, shell in next ch sp, skip next ch sp, sc in next ch sp, shell in next corner ch sp, sc in next ch sp, skip next ch sp*, shell in next ch sp; repeat between **, join with sl st in top of ch-3.

Rnd 5: Sl st in each of next 2 sts, (sl st, ch 3, sl st) in next ch sp, [*ch 4, (sl st, ch 3, sl st) in next sc or ch sp of next shell; repeat from * across to next corner, ch 3, skip next dc, sl st in next dc, ch 3, (sl st, ch 3, sl st, ch 4, sl st, ch 3, sl st) in next corner ch-3 sp, ch 3, skip next dc, sl st in next dc, ch 3, skip next dc, (sl st, ch 3, sl st) in next sc]; repeat between [ ] 3 more times, ch 4, join with sl st in first sc, fasten off.

Terrace Dreams

Continued from page 19

first ch, sc in next 7 chs, *skip next 2 chs, sc in next 8 chs, (sc, ch 2, sc) in next ch-2 sp, sc in next 8 chs; repeat from * 9 more times, skip next 2 chs, sc in last 8 chs, fasten off.

Rnd 180: Working around outer edge, join med. mint with sl st in first of row 178, ch 1, sc first 2 sts tog, ch 2, sc in same st, *[(ch 1, skip next st, sc in next st) 3 times, ch 1 skip next st, (sc, ch 2, sc) in next ch-2 sp], (ch 1, skip next st, sc in next st) 4 times, skip next 2 sts, sc in next st; repeat from * 9 more times; repeat between [ ], (ch 1, skip next st, sc in next st) 3 times, ch 1, skip next st, sc last 2 sts tog, ch 2, sc in same st; working in ends of rows, spacing sts so edge lays flat, (ch 1, sc) across to next corner, ch 1, (sc, ch 2, sc) in next st, (ch 1, skip next st, sc in next st) 3 times, ◊skip next 2 sts, sc in next st, (ch 1, skip next st, sc in next st) 3 times, ch 1, skip next st, (sc, ch 2, sc) in next st, (ch 1, skip next st, sc in next st) 4 times; repeat from ◊ 9 more times, skip next 2 sts, sc in next st, (ch 1, skip next st, sc in next st) 3 times, ch 2, sc in same st as last sc; working in ends of rows, spacing sts so edge lays flat, (ch 1, sc) across to next corner, ch 1, join with sl st in first sc, fasten off.

Rnd 181: Join med. lavender with sc in first corner ch-2 sp, ch 3, sc in same sp, ch 3, skip next st, *[(sc in next ch sp, ch 3, skip next st) 4 times, (sc, ch 3, sc) in next ch-2 sp, (ch 3, skip next st, sc in next ch sp) 4 times], skip next 2 sts*; repeat between ** 9 more times; repeat between [ ], ch 3, (sc ch 3, sc) in next corner ch sp, ◊ch 3, (sc, ch 3) in each ch sp across to next corner◊ ch-2 sp, (sc, ch 3, sc) in next corner ch sp, (ch 3, skip next st, sc in next ch sp) 3 times, skip next 2 sts; repeat between ** 10 more times, (sc in next ch sp, ch 3) 3 times, (sc, ch 3, sc) in next corner ch sp; repeat between ◊◊, join, fasten off.

Commemorate the seasons of your life
with lovingly crafted reminders handmade
especially for that meaningful occasion.
This exclusive selection of heartwarming
creations for special holidays or special
people lets you indulge those you love with
unforgettable offerings of exceptionally
good taste. Young and old alike will
delight in the inviting shades and textures
featured in these notable designs.

Celebration Magic

Mardi Gras

Finished Size: 45" x 54"
not including Tassels

Materials: Worsted-weight yarn — 14 oz. red, 10½ oz. each green, blue, orange, purple and yellow; K crochet hook or size needed to obtain gauge.

Gauge: With 2 strands held together,
1 dc = 1¼" tall; 5 hdc sts = 2"

Skill Level: ✧ Easy

STRIP NO. 1 (make 5)

Note: Work with 2 strands held together throughout.

Rnd 1: With purple, ch 123, sc in 3rd ch from hook, (hdc, sc, hdc) in same ch, *sc in next ch, (hdc in next ch, sc in next ch) across* to last ch, (hdc, sc, hdc, sc, hdc) in last ch; working on opposite side of ch, repeat between **, join with sl st in top of ch-2, fasten off (248 sts).

Rnd 2: Join yellow with sl st in first st, ch 3, dc in same st, *(ch 2, skip next st, 2 dc in next st) 2 times, (ch 1, skip next 2 sts, 2 dc in next st) 39 times, ch 1, skip next 2 sts*, 2 dc in next st; repeat between **, join with sl st in top of ch-3, fasten off.

Rnd 3: Join red with sl st in first ch sp, (ch 3, dc, ch 2, 2 dc) in same sp, *ch 1, (2 dc, ch 1, 2 dc) in next ch sp, (ch 1, 2 dc in next ch sp) 40 times, ch 1*, (2 dc, ch 2, 2 dc) in next ch sp; repeat between **, join, fasten off.

STRIP NO. 2 (make 4)

Rnd 1: With green, repeat same rnd of Strip No. 1.

Rnd 2: With orange, repeat same rnd of Strip No. 1.

Rnd 3: With blue, repeat same rnd of Strip No. 1.

ASSEMBLY

Starting with Strip No. 1 and alternating Strips No. 1 and No. 2, working through both thicknesses in **back lps** only, sew long edges together leaving 13 sts and chs on each end unsewn.

TASSEL (make 18, see Note)

Note: Make Tassels in following colors: four each of green, red and blue; two each of orange, yellow and purple.

For each Tassel, cut 50 strands each 20" long. Tie separate strand of same color tightly around middle of all strands; fold strands in half. Wrap another 20" strand around folded strands 2" from top of fold, covering ½"; secure and hide ends inside Tassel. Trim all ends evenly.

Beginning at left-hand Strip on one end of Afghan, tie one Tassel to end of each Strip in following color sequence: blue, red, green, purple, yellow, red, orange, blue, green.

Repeat on opposite end of Strips.

Easter Discovery

Finished Size: 43" x 54"

Materials: Worsted-weight yarn — 21 oz. off-white,
4 oz. each peach, aqua and lavender;
H crochet hook or size needed to obtain gauge.

Gauge: 7 dc = 2"; 1 dc row and 1 sc row = 1".

Skill Level: ✧ Easy

AFGHAN

Row 1: With off-white, ch 152, sc in 2nd ch from hook, sc in each ch across, turn (151 sc).

Row 2: Ch 3, dc in each st across, turn.

Row 3: Ch 1, sc in first st, (ch 2, skip next 2 sts, dc in next st, ch 2, skip next 2 sts, sc in next st) across, turn, fasten off.

Note: For **shell,** 5 dc in next st.

Row 4: Join peach with sl st in first st, ch 3, 2 dc in same st, sc in next dc, (shell in next sc, sc in next dc) across to last st, 3 dc in last st, turn, fasten off.

Note: For **long dc (ldc),** working over sc on last row, yo, insert hook in next dc on row before last, yo, draw up long lp, (yo, draw through 2 lps on hook) 2 times.

Row 5: Join off-white with sc in first st, ch 2, ldc, (ch 2, sc in center st of next shell, ch 2, ldc) across to last 3 dc, ch 2, sc in last st, turn.

Row 6: Ch 3, dc in each st and 2 dc in each ch-2 sp across, turn (151 dc).

Row 7: Repeat row 3.

Row 8: Join aqua with sl st in first st, ch 3, 2 dc in same st, sc in next dc, (shell in next sc, sc in next dc) across to last st, 3 dc in last st, turn, fasten off.

Rows 9-10: Repeat rows 5 and 6.

Row 11: Repeat row 3.

Row 12: Join lavender with sl st in first st, ch 3, 2 dc in same st, sc in next dc, (shell in next sc, sc in next dc) across to last st, 3 dc in last st, turn, fasten off.

Rows 13-14: Repeat rows 5 and 6.

Rows 15-122: Repeat rows 3-14 consecutively.

Row 123: Ch 1, sc in each st across, fasten off.🍃

Freedom Fantasy

Finished Size: 50" x 76"
not including Fringe

Materials: Worsted-weight yarn — 24 oz. each red,
white and blue; H crochet hook or size needed to obtain gauge.

Gauge: 1 shell = 1" tall; 1 shell and 1 sc = 2" across.

Skill Level: ✧✧ Average

STRIP (make 9)

Row 1: With white, ch 182, sc in 2nd ch from hook, (hdc in next ch, dc in next ch, hdc in next ch, sc in next ch) 45 times, ch 1; working on opposite side of starting ch, sc in first ch; repeat between ( ) 45 times, fasten off (362 sts).

Note: For **long sc (lsc),** working over sc of last rnd, insert hook in next ch of starting ch, yo, draw up long lp, yo, draw through both lps on hook.

Row 2: Join blue with lsc in first ch, (sc in each of next 3 sts on last rnd, lsc) 45 times leaving remaining sts unworked, **do not** turn, fasten off.

Note: For **shell,** (2 dc, ch 1, 2 dc) in next st.

Row 3: Join red with sl st in first st, ch 3, dc in same st, (skip next st, sc in next st, skip next st, shell in next st) across to last 4 sts, skip next st, sc in next st, skip next st, 2 dc in last st, fasten off.

Row 4: Join white with sc in first st, (shell in next sc, sc in ch sp of next shell) 44 times, shell in next sc, sc in last st, fasten off.

Rows 5-7: Working in unworked sts of row 1, repeat rows 2-4.

ASSEMBLY

To **join Strips,** holding two Strips wrong sides together, join blue with sc in first st on one long edge of first Strip, ch 2, sc in first st on one long edge of other Strip, (ch 2, sc in next shell on this Strip, ch 2, sc in next shell on other Strip, ch 2, sc in next sc on this Strip, ch 2, sc in next sc on other Strip) across, fasten off.

Continue to join all Strips in this manner.

FRINGE

For **each Fringe,** cut eight strands each 12" long. With all strands held together, fold in half, insert hook in end of row, draw fold through, draw all loose ends through fold, tighten. Trim ends.

Alternating white and blue, evenly space 19 Fringe across each short end of Afghan.

Love's Tryst

Finished Size: 50" x 60"

Materials: Worsted-weight yarn — 87 oz. white;
tapestry needle; G crochet hook or size needed to obtain gauge.

Gauge: 4 sc sts = 1"; 4 sc rows = 1".
Each Motif is 4½" square.

Skill Level: ✧ Easy

MOTIF (make 162)

Note: Circle portion of Motif has doubled thickness.

Rnd 1: For **circle,** ch 5, sl st in first ch to form ring, ch 3, 15 dc in ring, join with sl st in top of ch-3 (16 dc).

Rnd 2: Ch 3, dc in same st, 2 dc in each st around, join (32).

Rnd 3: Ch 3, dc in next 6 sts, (dc, ch 3, dc) in next st, *dc in next 7 sts, (dc, ch 3, dc) in next st; repeat from * around, join (36 dc, 4 ch-3 sps).

Rnd 4: Skipping ch-3 sps, ch 3, dc in each dc around, join.

Rnd 5: For **back side of circle,** ch 1, sc first 2 sts tog, (sc next 2 sts tog) around, join with sl st in first sc (18 sc).

Rnd 6: Ch 3, dc in each st around, join with sl st in top of ch-3.

Rnd 7: Ch 1, sc first 2 sts tog, (sc next 2 sts tog) around, join with sl st in first sc, fasten off (9 sc).

Rnd 8: Flatten Motif, with rnd 1 facing you, working in ch-3 sps on rnd 3, join with sc in any sp, ch 2, sc in same sp, ch 9, *(sc, ch 2, sc) in next ch-3 sp, ch 9; repeat from * around, join with sl st in first sc (8 sc, 4 ch-2 sps, 4 ch-9 sps).

Rnd 9: Ch 3, 5 dc in next ch-2 sp, dc in next sc, 9 dc in next ch-9 sp, (dc in next sc, 5 dc in next ch-2 sp, dc in next sc, 9 dc in next ch-9 sp) around, join with sl st in top of ch-3, fasten off.

ASSEMBLY

Holding Motifs wrong sides together, matching sts, sew together through **backs lps** according to Assembly Diagram. ❧

ASSEMBLY DIAGRAM

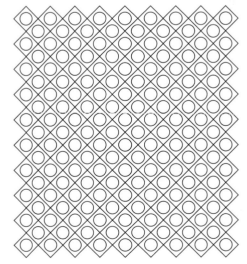

Miraculous Blessing

Finished Size: 37" x 40"
not including Fringe

Materials: Worsted-weight yarn — 18 oz. white, 9 oz. pink and 7 oz. blue; G crochet hook or size needed to obtain gauge.

Gauge: 1 shell = 1"; 2 shell rows and 1 sc row = 2".

Skill Level: ✦ Easy

AFGHAN

Note: For **shell,** 5 dc in next ch or st.

Row 1: With white, ch 139, 3 dc in 4th ch from hook, (skip next 2 chs, sc in next ch, skip next 2 chs, shell in next ch) across to last 3 chs, skip next 2 chs, sc in last ch, turn (22 shells).

Row 2: Ch 3, 3 dc in first st, (sc in center st of next shell, shell in next sc) across to last 4 sts, skip next 3 sts, sc in last st, turn, fasten off.

Row 3: Join pink with sl st in first st, ch 3, 3 dc in same st, (sc in center st of next shell, shell in next sc) across to last 4 sts, sc in last st, turn.

Row 4: Repeat row 2.

Row 5: With white, repeat row 3.

Rows 6-8: Ch 3, 3 dc in first st, (sc in center st of next shell, shell in next sc) across to last 4 sts, sc in last st, turn. At end of last row, fasten off.

Rows 9-10: With blue, repeat rows 3 and 2.

Rows 11-14: Repeat rows 5-8.

Rows 15-78: Repeat rows 3-14 consecutively, ending with row 6.

Row 79: Ch 1, sc in first st, (ch 2, sc in center st of next shell, ch 2, sc in next sc) across to last 4 sts, ch 2, sc in last st, fasten off.

FRINGE

For **each Fringe,** cut one 14" strand each color. With all strands held together, fold in half, insert hook in st, draw fold through st, draw all loose ends through fold, tighten. Trim ends.

Fringe 46 sts evenly spaced on each short end of Afghan.

Peppermint Swirls

Finished Size: 46" x 68"
not including Fringe

Materials: Worsted-weight yarn — 36 oz. white
and 35 oz. red; G crochet hook or size needed to obtain gauge.

Gauge: 4 sc sts = 1"; 4 sc rnds = 1".
Each Block is 5½" square.

Skill Level: ✧✧ Average

FIRST ROW
First Block

Rnd 1: With white, ch 6, sl st in first ch to form ring, ch 4, 27 tr in ring, join with sl st in top of ch-4, fasten off (28 tr).

Rnd 2: Working this rnd in **back lps** only, join red with sc in first st, sc in same st, (sc in next 6 sts, 2 sc in next st) 3 times, sc in last 6 sts, join with sl st in first sc, fasten off (32 sc).

Rnd 3: Join white with sc in first st, ch 3, skip next st, (sc in next st, ch 3, skip next st) around, join, fasten off (16 sc, 16 ch sps).

Rnd 4: Join red with sl st in first ch sp, ch 6, dc in same sp, (ch 3, sc in next ch sp) 3 times, ch 3, *(dc, ch 3, dc) in next ch sp, (ch 3, sc in next ch sp) 3 times, ch 3; repeat from * around, join with sl st in 3rd ch of ch-6, fasten off (20 ch sps, 12 sc, 8 dc).

Rnd 5: Join white with sc in corner ch sp between dc, ch 3, sc in same sp, (ch 3, sc in next ch sp) 4 times, ch 3, *(sc, ch 3, sc) in next corner ch sp, (ch 3, sc in next ch sp) 4 times, ch 3; repeat from * around, join with sl st in first sc.

Note: For **double treble crochet (dtr)** *(see fig. 8, pg. 157)*, yo 3 times, insert hook in next st, yo, draw lp through, (yo, draw through 2 lps on hook) 4 times.

Rnd 6: Sl st in next ch sp, ch 1, (sc, ch 3, sc) in same sp, 2 sc in next ch sp, dtr around post *(see fig. 14, page 158)* of corresponding tr on rnd 1 (tr that 2 sc are worked in), *[3 sc in next ch sp on this rnd, skip next tr on rnd 1, dtr around post of each of next 3 tr, skip next ch sp on this rnd, 3 sc in next ch sp, skip next tr on rnd 1, dtr around post of next tr, 2 sc in next ch sp on this rnd], (sc, ch 3, sc) in next ch sp, 2 sc in next ch sp, dtr around post of next tr on rnd 1; repeat from * 2 more times; repeat between [ ], join, fasten off.

Rnd 7: Join red with sc in first corner ch sp, ch 3, sc in same sp, sc in each st around with (sc, ch 3, sc) in each corner ch sp, join (19 sc on each side between corner ch sps).

Rnd 8: Sl st in next ch sp, ch 1, (sc, ch 3, sc) in same sp, *[(ch 3, skip next 2 sts, sc in next st) 6 times, ch 3, skip next st], (sc, ch 3, sc) in next corner ch sp; repeat from * 2 more times; repeat between [ ], join, fasten off.

Second Block

Rnds 1-7: Repeat same rnds of First Block.

Rnd 8: Sl st in next ch sp, ch 1, sc in same sp; holding Blocks wrong sides together, to **join,** ch 1, sl st in 2nd ch of corner ch sp on

Continued on page 42

Feliz Navidad

Finished Size: 44" x 68"
not including Fringe

Materials: Worsted-weight yarn — 40 oz. black,
14 oz. green and 10 oz. red; 218 each red and green 6 x 9-mm
pony beads; H crochet hook or size needed to obtain gauge.

Gauge: 7 dc sts = 2"; 2 dc rnds = 1¼".

Skill Level: ◇◇◇ Challenging

LARGE MOTIF (make 50)

Note: For **picot,** ch 8, sl st in 8th ch from hook.

For **joined picot,** ch 3, sl st in last picot, ch 4, sl st in first ch of ch-3.

Rnd 1: With black, ch 6, sl st in first ch to form ring, ch 3, 2 dc in ring, drop black, pick up green, picot, drop green, pick up black, ch 1; working over green, (3 dc in ring, drop black, pick up green, picot, drop green, pick up black, ch 1) around, join with sl st in top of ch-3 (18 dc, 6 picots).

Note: For **V-st,** (dc, ch 2, dc) in next st.

Rnd 2: Keeping picots to front, ch 3, dc in same st, V-st in next st, 2 dc in next st, drop black, pick up green, picot 3 times, drop green, pick up black, ch 1, (*2 dc in next st, V-st in next st, 2 dc in next st, drop black, pick up green, joined picot*, picot 2 times, drop green, pick up black, ch 1) 4 times; repeat between **, picot, ch 3, sl st in first picot of this rnd, ch 4, sl st in first ch of last ch-3 made, drop green, pick up black, ch 1, join.

Rnd 3: Working behind picots, ch 3, dc in each of next 2 sts, dc in next ch sp, sl st in back strand of joining sl st of joined picots, dc in same ch sp as last dc, dc in each of next 3 sts, drop black, pick up red, picot 3 times, drop red, pick up black, ch 1, (dc in each of next 3 sts, dc in next ch sp, sl st in back strand of joining sl st of joined picots, dc in same ch sp as

last dc, dc in each of next 3 sts, drop black, pick up red, picot 3 times, drop red, pick up black, ch 1) around, join.

Note: Pull unjoined center green picot of any 3-picot group on rnd 2 through picot below on rnd 1; pull center red picot on rnd 3 through center green picot. Repeat on each group of picots.

Rnd 4: Sl st in each of next 2 sts, ch 3, dc in next st, *[dc in next sl st, dc in each of next 2 sts; working on red picots, (sl st in **back lp** of 4th ch on next picot, ch 3) 2 times, sl st in **back lp** of 4th ch on next picot], skip next 2 dc, dc in each of next 2 sts; repeat from * 4 more times; repeat between [ ], join.

Rnd 5: Ch 1, sc in first 5 dc, sc in next sl st, 2 sc in next ch sp, (sc, ch 2, sc) in next sl st, 2 sc in next ch sp, sc in next sl st, *sc in next 5 dc, sc in next sl st, 2 sc in next ch sp, (sc, ch 2, sc) in next sl st, 2 sc in next ch sp, sc in next sl st; repeat from * around, join with sl st in first sc, fasten off (78 sc, 6 ch-2 sps).

Assembly

Holding two Motifs right sides together, matching sts, working through both thicknesses in **front lps,** with black, sl st 13 sts together from one ch sp to next ch sp, fasten off.

Continue joining Motifs until you have five strips of ten Motifs each.

Continued on page 43

Peppermint Swirls

Continued from page 38

other Block, ch 1, sc in same ch sp as last sc on this Block, (ch 1, sl st in 2nd ch of next ch-3 on other Block, ch 1, skip next 2 sts on this Block, sc in next st) 6 times, ch 1, sl st in 2nd ch of next ch-3 on other Block, ch 1, sc in next corner ch sp on this Block, ch 1, sc in 2nd ch of next corner ch sp on other Block, ch 1, sc in same ch sp as last sc on this Block, *[(ch 3, skip next 2 sts, sc in next st) 6 times, ch 3, skip next st], (sc, ch 3, sc) in next corner ch sp; repeat from *; repeat between [ ], join, fasten off.

Repeat Second Block 10 more times for a total of 12 Blocks on this row.

SECOND ROW
First Block
Joining to bottom of First Block on last Row, work same as Second Block of First Row.

Second Block
Rnds 1-7: Repeat same rnds of First Block on First Row.

Rnd 8: Sl st in next ch sp, ch 1, sc in same sp; holding Blocks wrong sides together, to **join,** ch 1, sl st in 2nd ch of corner ch sp on other Block, ch 1, sc in same ch sp as last sc on this Block, *(ch 1, sl st in 2nd ch of next ch-3 on other Block, ch 1, skip next 2 sts on this Block, sc in next st) 6 times, ch 1, sl st in 2nd ch of next ch-3 on other Block, ch 1, sc in next corner ch sp on this Block, ch 1, sc in 2nd ch of next corner ch sp on other Block, ch 1, sc in same ch sp as last sc on this Block,

repeat from *, (ch 3, skip next 2 sts, sc in next st) 6 times, ch 3, skip next st, join, fasten off.

Repeat Second Motif 10 more times for a total of 12 Motifs.

REMAINING ROWS
Repeat Second Row 6 more times for a total of 8 Rows.

BORDER
Rnd 1: Working around entire outer edge, join red with sc in any corner ch sp, 4 sc in same sp, (2 sc in each ch sp, sc in st on each side of seam and sc in each seam) around with 5 sc in each corner ch sp, join with sl st in first sc.

Rnd 2: Ch 1, sc in each st around with 3 sc in each center corner st, join, fasten off.

Rnd 3: Join white with sc in any st, sc in each st around with 3 sc in each center corner st, join, fasten off.

Rnd 4: Join red with sc in any st, sc in each st around with 3 sc in each center corner st, join, **do not** fasten off.

Rnd 5: Ch 1, sc in each st around with 3 sc in each center corner st, join, fasten off.

FRINGE
For **each Fringe,** cut two strands red each 14" long. With both strands held together, fold in half, insert hook in st, draw fold through st, draw all loose ends through fold, tighten. Trim ends.

Fringe in each st on each short end of Afghan.

Feliz Navidad

Continued from page 40

SMALL MOTIF STRIP (make 4)
First Motif

Rnd 1: With black, ch 6, sl st in first ch to form ring, ch 3, 2 dc in ring, drop black, pick up green, picot 3 times, drop green, pick up black, ch 1, (3 dc in ring, drop black, pick up green, picot 3 times, drop green, pick up black, ch 1) around, join with sl st in top of ch-3 (12 dc, 12 picots).

Rnd 2: Ch 3, dc in each of next 2 sts, (sl st in **back lp** of 4th ch on next picot, ch 3) 2 times, sl st in **back lp** of 4th ch on next picot], *dc in each of next 3 sts, (sl st in **back lp** of 4th ch on next picot, ch 3) 2 times, sl st in **back lp** of 4th ch on next picot; repeat from * around, join.

Rnd 3: Ch 2, *dc in each of next 2 dc, dc in next sl st, 3 dc in next ch sp, (tr, ch 2, tr) in next sl st, 3 dc in next ch sp, dc in next sl st, dc in each of next 2 dc, hdc in next dc, hdc in next sl st, 3 sc in next ch sp, (sc, ch 2, sc) in next sl st, 3 sc in next ch sp, hdc in next sl st*, hdc in next dc; repeat between ** join with sl st in top of ch-2, fasten off (52 sts, 4 ch-2 sps).

Second Motif

Rnds 1-2: Repeat same rnds of First Motif.

Rnd 3: Ch 2, dc in each of next 2 dc, dc in next sl st, 3 dc in next ch sp, tr in next sl st, ch 1, sl st in ch-2 sp between tr on last Small Motif, ch 1, tr in same sl st as last tr, *3 dc in next ch sp, dc in next sl st, dc in each of next 2 dc, hdc in next dc, hdc in next sl st, 3 sc in next ch sp, (sc, ch 2, sc) in next sl st, 3 sc in next ch sp, hdc in next sl st*, hdc in next dc, dc in each of next 2 dc, dc in next sl st, 3 dc in next ch sp, (tr, ch 2, tr) in next sl st; repeat between **, join with sl st in top of ch-2, fasten off (52 sts, 4 ch-2 sps).

Repeat Second Motif 7 more times, for a total of 9 Motifs.

ASSEMBLY

Holding Strips right sides together, alternating Large Motifs and Small Motifs, working through both thicknesses in **front lps** only, with black, sl st Strips together.

FRINGE

Notes: For **Fringe,** ch 10, drop lp from hook, pull lp through hole on bead, ch 1, sl st in 2nd ch from hook, sl st in each ch across.

Alternate red and green beads when working Fringe.

With right side facing you, working around entire outer edge in **back lps** only, join black with sl st in st before any seam, sl st same st and st on other side of seam together, sl st in next st, Fringe, (sl st in each of next 2 sts or chs, Fringe) across to one st before next seam, *sl st sts on each side of seam together, sl st in next st, Fringe, (sl st in each of next 2 sts or chs, Fringe) across to one st before next seam; repeat from * around, join with sl st in first sl st, fasten off.

Imagine sinking effortlessly into a
downy pile of cozy blankets and throws for
a few hours of satisfying relaxation.
Re-create the carefree feeling of a weekend
in the country with mellow designs
reminiscent of patchwork quilts and
colorful comforters. Lend an air of
unhurried pleasure to your favorite corner
of the world with any of these appealing
selections as your personal companion.

Charming Comforts

Country Fair

Finished Size: 49" x 69"
not including Fringe

Materials: Worsted-weight yarn — 57 oz. white;
sport-weight yarn — 5½ oz. blue and 4 oz. red; tapestry needle; G
crochet and H afghan hooks or sizes needed to obtain gauges.

Gauge: G hook, 4 sts = 1". H afghan hook,
4 afghan sts = 1"; 7 afghan st rows = 2".

Skill Level: ✧✧ Average

PANEL (make 4)

Row 1: With G hook and white, ch 50, sc in 2nd ch from hook, sc in each ch across, turn (49 sc).

Row 2: Ch 1, sc in each st across, turn.

Row 3: Drop lp from hook, pick up lp with H afghan hook (loop on hook counts as first st), skip first sc, draw up lp in next st and in each st across leaving all lps on hook; to **work sts off hook,** yo, draw through one lp on hook (*see ill. A, fig. 16, page 159*), (yo, draw through 2 lps on hook) across leaving one lp on hook at end of row (*see ill. B*).

Row 4: For **afghan st,** skip first vertical bar, *insert hook under next vertical bar (*see ill. C*), yo, draw lp through; repeat from * across to last vertical bar; for **last st,** insert hook under last bar and st directly behind it (*see ill. D*), yo, draw lp through; work sts off hook.

Rows 5-241: Work in afghan st.

Row 242: Drop lp from hook, pick up lp with G crochet hook, sc in each vertical bar across, turn (49 sc).

Row 243: Ch 1, sc in each st across, fasten off.

With red and blue, using Cross Stitch (*see ill. on page 58*), skip first 5 rows, embroider star over next 41 rows according to graph; (skip next 7 rows and embroider star over next 41 rows) 4 times.

ASSEMBLY

For first, second and third Panels, with G hook and white, join with sc in top left-hand corner, sc in end of each row across, fasten off.

For second, third and fourth Panels, with G hook and white, join with sc in bottom right-hand corner, sc in end of each row across, fasten off.

To **join,** hold two Panels wrong sides together, matching sts on long edges; working through both thicknesses, with G hook and white, join with sl st in first st, (ch 1, sl st) in each st across, fasten off.

Join Panels with unworked edges of first and fourth Panels on outside edges.

BORDER

Rnd 1: With G hook and white, join with sc in any st, sc in each st around with 3 sc in each corner, join with sl st in first sc.

Rnd 2: Working this rnd in **back lps** (*see fig. 1, page 156*) only, ch 1, sc in each st around, join, fasten off.

Rnd 3: Working in **front lps** of rnd 1, join red with sl st in any st, ch 1, (sl st, ch 1) in each st around, join with sl st in first sl st, fasten off.

FRINGE

For **each Fringe,** cut 3 strands white each 14" long. With all three strands held together, fold in half, insert hook in st, draw fold through st,

Continued on page 58

Burgundy Lilies

Finished Size: 45" x 58"

Materials: Worsted-weight yarn — 25 oz. lt. rust,
17 oz. each dk. and pale rust and 10 oz. med rust; tapestry needle;
I crochet hook or size needed to obtain gauge.

Gauge: 2 dc sts = 1"; 1 dc row = 1".

Skill Level: ✧✧ Average

FIRST BLOCK (make 18)

Note: Work with 2 strands held together throughout entire pattern unless otherwise stated.

Rnd 1: With pale rust, ch 6, sl st in first ch to form ring, ch 3, 2 dc in ring, ch 12, (3 dc in ring, ch 12) 3 times, join with sl st in top of ch-3, fasten off (12 dc, 4 ch lps).

Rnd 2: Working in sps between sts, join lt. rust with sl st in sp between first 2 sts, ch 3, 2 dc in same sp, ch 1, 3 dc in next sp, ch 12, skip next ch lp, (3 dc in next sp, ch 1, 3 dc in next sp, ch 12, skip next ch lp) around, join, fasten off.

Rnd 3: Join med. rust with sl st in sp between first 2 sts, ch 3, 2 dc in same sp, ch 1, 3 dc in next ch-1 sp, ch 1, skip next sp between sts, 3 dc in next sp, ch 12, skip next ch lp, (3 dc in sp between next 2 sts, ch 1, 3 dc in next ch-1 sp, ch 1, skip next sp between sts, 3 dc in next sp, ch 12, skip next ch lp) around, join, fasten off.

Note: For each corner, pull ch lp on rnd 2 from bottom to top through ch lp on rnd 1, pull chain lp on rnd 3 from bottom to top through ch lp on rnd 2.

Rnd 4: Join dk. rust with sl st in sp between first 2 sts, ch 3, 2 dc in same sp, 3 dc in each of next 2 ch-1 sps, skip next sp between sts, 3 dc in next sp, (3 sc, ch 2, 3 sc) in next ch-12 lp, *3 dc in next sp between sts, 3 dc in each of next 2 ch-1 sps, skip next sp between sts, 3 dc in next sp, (3 sc, ch 2, 3 sc) in next ch-12 lp, join, fasten off.

SECOND BLOCK (make 17)

Rnd 1: With dk. rust, repeat same rnd of First Block.

Rnd 2: With med. rust, repeat same rnd of First Block.

Rnd 3: With lt. rust, repeat same rnd of First Block.

Rnd 4: With pale rust, repeat same rnd of First Block.

For first, third and fifth strips, holding Blocks wrong sides together, alternating First and Second Blocks and starting with First Block, sew seven blocks together through **back lps** *(see fig. 1, page 156)*.

For second and fourth strips, holding Blocks wrong sides together, alternating Second and First Blocks and starting with Second Block, sew seven blocks together through **back lps.**

EDGING

Join lt. rust with sl st in any st on first strip, ch 3, dc in each st and in each ch-2 sp on each side of seam around with 3 dc in each corner ch-2 sp, join with sl st in top of ch-3, fasten off.

Repeat on remaining strips.

Holding strips wrong sides together, with one strand, sew long edges together through **back lps.**

BORDER

Join med. rust with sl st in any st, ch 3, dc in each st around with 3 dc in each center corner st, join with sl st in top of ch-3, fasten off.🍂

Texas Starburst

Finished Size: 48" x 56"

Materials: Worsted-weight yarn — 24 oz. soft white,
7 oz. each purple variegated, rust variegated and green variegated,
5 oz. each purple, blue, lt. rust, plum, green, red and blue-green;
yarn bobbins (optional); F crochet and G afghan extension
hooks or sizes needed to obtain gauges.

Gauge: F hook, 9 sc = 2"; 9 sc rows = 2".
G afghan hook, 9 afghan sts = 2"; 4 afghan st rows = 1".

Skill Level: ✧✧ Average

AFGHAN

Row 1: With afghan hook and white, ch 216; leaving all lps on hook, insert hook in 2nd ch from hook, yo, draw lp through, (insert hook in next ch, yo, draw lp through) across, **do not** turn; to **work sts off hook,** yo, draw through one lp on hook (*see ill. A, fig. 16, page 159*), (yo, draw through 2 lps on hook) across leaving one lp on hook at end of row (*see ill. B*), **do not** turn.

Row 2: For **afghan st,** skip first vertical bar, *insert hook under next vertical bar (*see. ill. C*), yo, draw lp through; repeat from * across to last vertical bar; for **last st,** insert hook under last bar and st directly behind it (*see ill. D*), yo, draw lp through; work sts off hook (216 sts).

Rows 3-8: Work in afghan st.

Notes: For **afghan st color change,** drop current color, insert hook under next vertical bar, yo with next color, draw lp through; to work sts off hook, (work until one lp of current color remains on hook, drop current color, pick up next color from under first color, yo, draw through 2 lps on hook) across.

Do not carry yarn across back of work for more than 2 or 3 sts, use new bobbin for each section of color. Always pick up next color from under current color to prevent a gap from forming.

Row 9: For **first color change row,** changing colors according to graphs on pages 60 and 61, afghan st 59; (with purple; afghan st one); with new skein white, afghan st 96; repeat between ( ); with white, afghan st 59; work sts off hook.

Rows 10-106: Work in afghan st changing colors according to graph.

Rows 107-212: Turning graph upside down, work remaining rows according to graph. At end of last row, fasten off.

BORDER

Notes: Work Border alternating each color except white.

Do not join rnds unless otherwise stated. Mark first st of each rnd.

Rnd 1: With F hook and purple, join with sc in first st, sc in next 6 sts changing to next color (*see fig. 9, page 158*) in last st made, (sc in next 7 sts changing to next color in last st made) across to last 6 sts, sc in next 5 sts, 2 sc in last st changing to next color in last st made, sc in same st; *working in ends of rows, skip first row, (sc in next 7 rows changing to next color in last st made) across to last 8 rows, sc in next 7 rows, skip last row*; working on opposite side of starting ch, sc in first ch changing to next color in last st made, 2 sc in same ch, sc in next 5 chs changing to next color in last st made, (sc in next 7 chs changing to next color in last st made) across, 2 sc in same st; repeat between **, 2 sc in first st.

Rnds 2-7: Following established color sequence, (sc in each st across to 2 sts before

Continued on page 60

Calico Patchwork

Finished Size: 64" x 75"

Materials: Worsted-weight yarn — 25 oz. variegated, 18 oz. white, 14 oz. pink, 7 oz. each lavender and green; I crochet hook or size needed to obtain gauge.

Gauge: 3 dc sts = 1"; 3 dc rows = 2".

Skill Level: ✧✧ Average

BLOCK (make 12)

Row 1: With pink, ch 68, dc in 4th ch from hook, dc in each ch across, turn (66 dc).

Notes: Each square on graph equals 2 dc.

When changing colors (*see fig. 10, page 158*), always drop yarn to wrong side of work. Use a separate skein of yarn for each color section. Do not carry yarn across from one section to another. Fasten off colors at end of each color section.

Beginning ch-3 is used and counted as first st of each row.

Work odd-numbered graph rows from right to left and even numbered rows from left to right.

Row 2: For row 2 of graph, ch 3, dc in next st changing to variegated, dc in next 28 sts changing to pink in last st made, dc in each of next 2 sts changing to white in last st made, dc

Continued on page 59

☐ = Variegated
☐ = White
■ = Lavender
▓ = Pink
▒ = Green

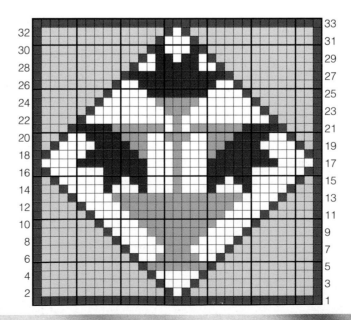

Trailing Petals

Finished Size: 60" x 72"
not including Fringe

Materials: Worsted-weight yarn — 46 oz. dk. rose,
10 oz. each lt. rose and pale pink, 6 oz. rose/blue variegated;
J crochet hook or size needed to obtain gauge.

Gauge: 5 dc sts = 2"; 1 cluster = 1" tall.

Skill Level: ✧✧ Average

AFGHAN

Row 1: With dk. rose, ch 170, sc in 2nd ch from hook, sc in each ch across, turn (169 sc).

Row 2: Ch 1, sc in first st, (dc in next st, sc in next st) across, turn.

Row 3: Ch 3, (sc in next st, dc in next st) across, turn.

Rows 4-19: Repeat rows 2 and 3 alternately.

Row 20: Ch 3, dc in each st across, turn, fasten off.

Note: For **cluster (cl),** yo, insert hook in next st, yo, draw lp through, yo, draw through 2 lps on hook, (yo, insert hook in same st, yo, draw lp through, yo, draw through 2 lps on hook) 3 times, yo, draw through all 5 lps on hook.

Row 21: Join lt. rose with sl st in first st, ch 4, skip next 2 sts, (cl in next st, ch 1, skip next st) across to last 2 sts, skip next st, dc in last st, **do not** turn, fasten off (82 cls, 2 dc). First ch-4 counts as one dc and one ch.

Row 22: Join pale pink with sl st in first st, ch 4, (cl, ch 1) in each ch-1 sp across, dc in last st, turn, fasten off (83 cls, 2 dc).

Row 23: Join dk. rose with sc in first st, sc in each st and in each ch-1 sp across, **do not** turn (169 sc).

Row 24: Join variegated with sc in first st; for **cable,** (ch 3, skip next 2 sts, sc in next st, **turn,** sc in each of next 3 chs, sl st in next st, **turn;** working behind ch-3, sc in each of next 2 skipped sts) across, sl st in last st, **turn,** fasten off (56 cables).

Row 25: Join dk. rose with sc in first st,

evenly sp 168 more sc across, **do not** turn, fasten off.

Row 26: Join pale pink with sl st in first st, ch 3, (cl in next st, ch 1, skip next st) across to last 2 sts, cl in next st, dc in last st, **do not** turn, fasten off (84 cls. 2 dc).

Row 27: Join lt. rose with sl st in first st, ch 4, skip next cl, (cl, ch 1) in each ch-1 sp across, dc in last st, turn, fasten off (83 cls, 2 dc).

Row 28: Join dk. rose with sl st in first st, ch 3, dc in each ch-1 sp and in each st across, turn (169 dc).

Rows 29-45: Repeat rows 2 and 3 alternately, ending with row 2.

Rows 46-123: Repeat rows 20-45 consecutively.

Row 124: Repeat row 3, **do not** turn, fasten off.

Row 125: For **edging,** join dk. rose with sc in first st, sc in each st across, **do not** turn; working in ends of rows, spacing sts so edge lays flat, sc across, fasten off.

Row 126: For **edging,** join dk. rose with sc in end of row 1; working in ends of rows, spacing sts so edge lays flat, sc across, fasten off.

Row 127: Join lt. rose with sl st in first st on one edging, ch 3, hdc in same st, *skip next st, (hdc, ch 1, hdc) in next st; repeat from * across, **do not** turn, fasten off. First ch-3 counts as hdc and ch 1.

Row 128: Join pale pink with sl st in first ch-1 sp, ch 2, hdc in same sp, 2 hdc in each ch-

Continued on page 59

Vineyard Harvest

Finished Size: 58" x 74"
not including Fringe

Materials: Worsted-weight yarn — 50 oz. lavender,
8 oz. lt. purple and 5 oz. dk. purple; J crochet hook
or size needed to obtain gauge.

Gauge: 5 sts = 2"; 2 hdc rows = 1"; 1 dc = 1" tall.

Skill Level: ✧✧ Average

AFGHAN

Notes: For **horizontal cluster (h-cl),** ch 4, yo, insert hook in 3rd ch from hook, yo, draw lp through, yo, draw through 2 lps on hook, (yo, insert hook in same ch, yo, draw lp through, yo, draw through 2 lps on hook) 2 times, yo, draw through all 4 lps on hook.

For **dc next 4 sts tog,** (yo, insert hook in next st, yo, draw lp through, yo, draw through 2 lps on hook) 4 times, yo, draw through all 5 lps on hook.

Row 1: With lavender, ch 175, sc in 2nd ch from hook, sc in each ch across, **do not** turn, fasten off (174 sc).

Row 2: Join lavender with sl st in first st, ch 3, dc next 2 sts tog, h-cl, (dc next 4 sts tog, h-cl) across to last 3 sts, dc next 2 sts tog, dc in last st, turn. Back of row 2 is right side of work.

Row 3: Ch 3, 2 dc in next st, skip next h-cl, (4 dc in next dc, skip next h-cl) across to last 2 sts, 2 dc in next st, dc in last st, turn (174 dc).

Rows 4-13: Repeat rows 2 and 3 alternately.

Row 14: Ch 2, hdc in each st across, turn, fasten off.

Row 15: Join lt. purple with sl st in first st, ch 2, hdc in each st across, turn, fasten off.

Row 16: With dk. purple, repeat row 15.

Row 17: With lt. purple, repeat row 15, **do not** fasten off.

Row 18: Repeat row 14.

Note: For **cross stitch (cr st),** working in sts on last dk. purple row, skip next 14 dk. purple

sts, tr around post of next st, skip next st on last row behind tr, dc in next st; working in front of last tr, tr around 13th skipped dk. purple st, skip next st on last row behind tr.

Row 19: Join dk. purple with sl st in first st, ch 2, hdc in each of next 2 sts, tr around post of 6th st on last dk. purple row, skip next st on last row behind tr, dc in next st; working in front of last tr, tr around post of fourth st on last purple row, skip next st on last row behind tr, (dc in next 12 sts, cr st) 11 times, dc in each of last 3 sts, **do not** turn, fasten off.

Row 20: Join lt. purple with sl st in first st, ch 2, hdc in each st across, turn, fasten off (174 hdc).

Row 21: Join lavender with sl st in first st, ch 2, hdc in each st across, **do not** turn, fasten off.

Rows 22-80: Repeat rows 2-21 consecutively, ending with row 20.

Row 81: Working in starting ch on opposite side of row 1, with wrong side facing you, join lavender with sl st in first ch, ch 2, hdc in each ch across, turn, fasten off.

Rows 82-87: Repeat rows 15-20.

EDGING

Rnd 1: Working around outer edge, join lavender with sc in first st of row 80, sc in same st, sc in each st across with 2 sc in last st; (working in ends of rows, spacing sts so piece

Continued on page 59

Country Fair

Continued from page 46

draw all loose ends through fold, tighten. Trim ends.

Fringe in each st on each short end of Afghan.🍂

Continued from page 46

CROSS STITCH OVER AFGHAN STITCH ILLUSTRATION

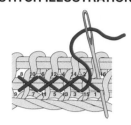

■ = Red Cross Stitch
■ = Blue Cross Stitch

STAR GRAPH

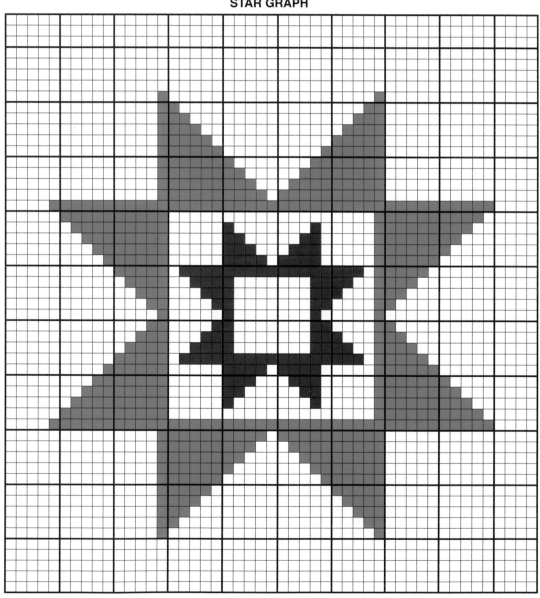

Calico Patchwork

Continued from page 52

in each of next 2 sts changing to pink in last st made, dc in each of next 2 sts changing to variegated in last st made, dc in next 28 sts changing to pink in last st made, dc in each of last 2 sts, turn.

Rows 3-33: Ch 3, dc in each st across changing colors according to graph, turn. At end of last row, fasten off.

Holding Blocks right sides together, matching sts, with pink, sew together in three rows of four Blocks each.

BORDER

Rnd 1: Working around outer edge, join pink with sc in first st, sc in each st and 2 sc in end of each row around, join with sl st in first sc, fasten off (198 sc on each short end, 264 sc on each long edge).

Rnd 2: Join white with sc in first st, ch 5, dc in same st, skip next st, *(sc, ch 3, dc) in next st, skip next st; repeat from * around with (sc, ch 5, dc) in each corner st, join with sl st in first sc, fasten off.&

Trailing Petals

Continued from page 55

1 sp across, fasten off.

Repeat rows 127 and 128 on opposite side of Afghan.

FRINGE

For **each Fringe,** cut 6 strands each 14" long. With all strands held together, fold in half, insert hook in st, draw fold through st, draw all loose ends through fold, tighten. Trim ends.

Fringe in every other st or row on each short end of Afghan matching color of row above.&

Vineyard Harvest

Continued from page 56

lays flat, sc across), 2 sc in first st of row 87, sc in each st across with 2 sc in last st; repeat between ( ), join with sl st in first sc.

Row 2: Sl st in next st, ch 3, dc in same st, *skip next 2 sts, (sl st, ch 3, dc) in next st; repeat from * 56 more times, skip next 2 sts, sl st in next st leaving remaining sts unworked, fasten off.

Row 3: Working on opposite side of Afghan, join with sl st in 2nd st of right-hand 2-sc group, ch 3, dc in same st, *skip next 2 sts, (sl st, ch 3, dc) in next st; repeat from * 56 more times, skip next 2 sts, sl st in next st leaving remaining sts unworked, fasten off.

FRINGE

For **each Fringe,** cut 3 strands each 14" long. With all strands held together, fold in half, insert hook in st, draw fold through st, draw all loose ends through fold, tighten. Trim ends.

Fringe in each st on each short end of Afghan, matching color of row above.&

Texas Starburst

Continued from page 51

next color section, sc in next st changing to next color) around with 3 sc in each center corner st. At end of last rnd, join with sl st in first sc, fasten off.

Graph is worked across two pages.

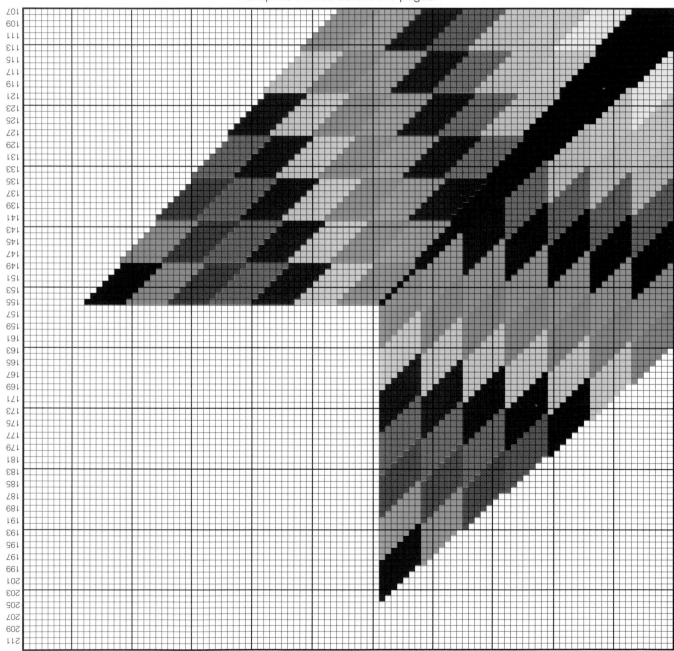

= Soft White
= Purple Variegated
= Rust Variegated
= Green Variegated
= Purple
= Blue

= Lt. Rust
= Plum
= Green
= Red
= Blue-Green

Graph is worked across two pages.

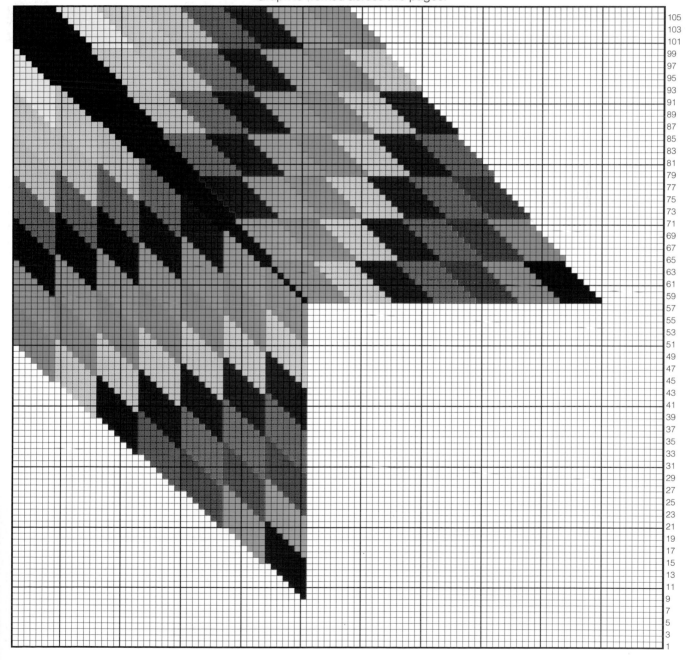

Feast your eyes on a banquet of
scrumptious delicacies in mouth-watering
colors and savory textures pretty enough
to please even the most discriminating
palate. A delectable medley of good taste,
these luscious concoctions will spice up
any decor with a flavor all their own.
Succulent, fruity hues drizzled with
creamy frosting will satisfy your craving
for appetizing appointments.

Delicious Temptations

Blueberry Ice

Finished Size: 50½" x 68"
not including Tassels

Materials: Worsted-weight yarn — 40 oz. white
and 10 oz. blue; H crochet hook or size needed to obtain gauge.

Gauge: 2 sc and 1 shell = 2"; 1 V-st row and 1 shell row = 2".

Skill Level: ✧✧ Average

FIRST STRIP

Notes: For **spike,** ch 4, sc in 2nd ch from hook, hdc in next ch, dc in last ch.

For **V-st,** (dc, ch 1, dc) in next st.

For **shell,** (2 dc, ch 1, 2 dc) in next ch sp.

Rnd 1: With white; for **base ch,** ch 162, sc in 2nd ch from hook, (spike, skip next 3 chs on base ch, sc in next ch) across, spike, sc in same ch on base as last sc; working on opposite side of base ch, repeat between ( ) across, spike, join with sl st in first sc, fasten off.

Rnd 2: Join blue with sc in tip of any spike on one long edge, V-st in each sc and sc in tip of each spike around with 5 sc in tip of spike on each end, join with sl st in first sc, fasten off.

Rnd 3: Join white with sc in 2nd sc of 5-sc group on one end, shell in next sc, sc in next sc, shell in ch sp of each V-st and sc in each sc across to next 5-sc group, sc in 2nd st of next 5-sc group, shell in next sc, sc in next sc, shell in ch sp of each V-st and sc in each sc across, join, fasten off.

SECOND STRIP

Rnds 1-2: Repeat same rnds of First Strip.

Rnd 3: Join white with sc in 2nd sc of 5-sc group on one end, shell in next sc, sc in next sc, shell in next V-st, (sc in next sc; for **joined shell,** 2 dc in next V-st, sl st in ch sp of corresponding shell on last Strip, 2 dc in same V-st) 39 times, sc in next sc, shell in next V-st, sc in 2nd sc of next 5-sc group, shell in next sc, sc in next sc, shell in ch sp of each V-st and sc in each sc across, join, fasten off.

Repeat Second Strip 9 more times for a total of 11 Strips.

TASSEL (make 12 blue, 10 white)

For each Tassel, cut 40 strands each 14" long. Tie separate strand tightly around middle of all strands; fold strands in half. Wrap 20" strand 1" from top of fold, covering ¾"; secure. Trim ends.

Alternating colors and beginning with blue, tie Tassels to ends of Strips.

BY SHEP SHEPHERD

Raspberry Sherbet

Finished Size: 41" x 65"
not including Fringe

Materials: Worsted-weight yarn — 30 oz. rose, 8 oz. black and 6 oz. white; I crochet hook or size needed to obtain gauge.

Gauge: 3 sts = 1"; 2 dc rows = 1¼".

Skill Level: ✧✧ Average

AFGHAN

Note: For **dc next 5 sts or chs tog,** (yo, insert hook in next st or ch, yo, draw lp through, yo, draw through 2 lps on hook) 5 times, yo, draw through all 6 lps on hook.

Rnd 1: With rose, ch 146, 2 dc in 4th ch from hook, (dc in next 5 chs, dc next 5 chs tog, dc in next 5 chs, 5 dc in next ch, dc in next 10 chs, dc next 5 chs tog, dc in next 10 chs, 5 dc in next ch) 3 times, dc in next 5 chs, dc next 5 chs tog, dc in next 5 chs, 3 dc in last ch, turn (143 dc).

Rows 2-7: Ch 3, 2 dc in same st, (dc in next 5 sts, dc next 5 sts tog, dc in next 5 sts, 5 dc in next st, dc in next 10 sts, dc next 5 sts tog, dc in next 10 sts, 5 dc in next st) 3 times, dc in next 5 sts, dc next 5 sts tog, dc in next 5 sts, 3 dc in last st, turn. At end of last row, fasten off.

Row 8: Join black with sl st in first st, ch 3, 2 dc in same st, (dc in next 5 sts, dc next 5 sts tog, dc in next 5 sts, 5 dc in next st, dc in next 10 sts, dc next 5 sts tog, dc in next 10 sts, 5 dc in next st) 3 times, dc in next 5 sts, dc next 5 sts tog, dc in next 5 sts, 3 dc in last st, turn, fasten off.

Row 9: Join white with sl st in first st, ch 3, 2 dc in same st, (dc in next 5 sts, dc next 5 sts tog, dc in next 5 sts, 5 dc in next st, dc in next 10 sts, dc next 5 sts tog, dc in next 10 sts, 5 dc in next st) 3 times, dc in next 5 sts, dc next 5 sts tog, dc in next 5 sts, 3 dc in last st, turn, fasten off.

Row 10: Repeat row 8.

Row 11: Join rose with sl st in first st, ch 3, 2 dc in same st, (dc in next 5 sts, dc next 5 sts tog, dc in next 5 sts, 5 dc in next st, dc in next 10 sts, dc next 5 sts tog, dc in next 10 sts, 5 dc in next st) 3 times, dc in next 5 sts, dc next 5 sts tog, dc in next 5 sts, 3 dc in last st, turn, fasten off.

Row 12: Repeat row 8.

Row 13: Join white with sl st in first st, ch 3, 2 dc in same st, (dc in next 5 sts, dc next 5 sts tog, dc in next 5 sts, 5 dc in next st, dc in next 10 sts, dc next 5 sts tog, dc in next 10 sts, 5 dc in next st) 3 times, dc in next 5 sts, dc next 5 sts tog, dc in next 5 sts, 3 dc in last st, turn, fasten off.

Row 14: Repeat row 8.

Row 15: Join rose with sl st in first st, ch 3, 2 dc in same st, (dc in next 5 sts, dc next 5 sts tog, dc in next 5 sts, 5 dc in next st, dc in next 10 sts, dc next 5 sts tog, dc in next 10 sts, 5 dc in next st) 3 times, dc in next 5 sts, dc next 5 sts tog, dc in next 5 sts, 3 dc in last st, turn, **do not** fasten off.

Rows 16-49: Ch 3, 2 dc in same st, (dc in next 5 sts, dc next 5 sts tog, dc in next 5 sts, 5 dc in next st, dc in next 10 sts, dc next 5 sts tog, dc in next 10 sts, 5 dc in next st) 3 times, dc in next 5 sts, dc next 5 sts tog, dc in next 5 sts, 3 dc in last st, turn. At end of last row, fasten off.

Continued on page 77

Petit Fours

Finished Size: 46½" x 66½"
not including Fringe

Materials: Worsted-weight yarn — 44 oz. pink, 28 oz. black and 5 oz. red; G crochet hook or size needed to obtain gauge.

Gauge: 4 sts = 1". Each Block is 5" square.

Skill Level: ✧ Easy

BLOCK (make 117)

Row 1: With red, ch 8, sl st in first ch to form ring, ch 1, sc in each ch around, join with sl st in first sc, fasten off (8 sc).

Rnd 2: Working in starting ch on opposite side of rnd 1, join pink with sl st in any ch, ch 3, 4 dc in same ch, ch 2, skip next ch, (5 dc in next ch, ch 2, skip next ch) around, join with sl st in top of ch-3 (20 dc).

Note: For **shell,** (5 dc, ch 2, 5 dc) in next ch sp.

Rnd 3: Sl st in next 4 sts, (sl st, ch 3, 4 dc, ch 2, 5 dc) in next ch sp, ch 1, (shell in next ch sp, ch 1) around, join.

Rnd 4: Sl st in next 4 sts, (sl st, ch 3, 4 dc, ch 2, 5 dc) in next ch sp, ch 1, 5 dc in next ch-1 sp, ch 1, (shell in next corner ch sp, ch 1, 5 dc in next ch-1 sp, ch 1) around, join, fasten off.

Rnd 5: Join black with sc in any st, sc in each st and in each ch-1 sp around with 3 sc in each corner ch sp, join with sl st in first sc, fasten off.

ASSEMBLY

To **join,** hold two Blocks wrong sides together, matching sts, working through both thicknesses in **back lps only,** join black with sl st in any center corner st, sl st in each st across to next center corner st, fasten off.

Continue joining Blocks in same manner, making nine rows of thirteen Blocks each.

EDGING

Rnd 1: Working around entire outer edge, join black with sc in any st, sc in each st around with 3 sc in each center corner st, join with sl st in first sc.

Rnd 2: Ch 1, sc in each st around with 3 sc in each center corner st, join.

Rnd 3: Ch 1, sc in first st, ch 3, skip next st, (sc in next st, ch 3, skip next st) around with 2 sc in each corner, join, fasten off.

FRINGE

For **each Fringe,** cut 5 strands each 14" long. With all strands held together, fold in half, insert hook in ch sp, draw fold through sp, draw all loose ends through fold, tighten. Trim ends.

Fringe in each ch sp on each short end of Afghan.❧

Ribbon Candy

Finished Size: 53" x 68"

Materials: Worsted-weight yarn — 50 oz. raspberry and 23 oz. jade; H crochet hook or size needed to obtain gauge.

Gauge: 7 sts = 2".

Skill Level: ✧✧ Average

STRIP (make 13)

Row 1: With raspberry, ch 3, sl st in first ch to form ring, ch 3, 6 dc in ring, turn (7 dc).

Note: For **front post stitch (fp)** *(see fig. 14, pg. 158)*, insert hook from right to left around post of st on previous row, complete as sc.

Row 2: Ch 1, fp around each st across, turn.

Row 3: Ch 3, skip next 2 sc, 7 dc in next sc, skip next 2 sc, dc in last sc, turn.

Row 4: Ch 1, skip first dc, fp around next 7 sts, dc in same st as ch-3 of previous row, turn.

Row 5: Ch 3, skip next 3 sc, 7 dc in next sc, skip next 2 sc, dc in last sc, turn.

Rows 6-149: Repeat rows 4 and 5 alternately. At end of last row, **do not** turn.

Rnd 150: Working around outer edge, sl st in end of next fp row, ch 3, 2 dc in same row, ch 1, (3 dc, ch 1) in end of each fp row across; working in beginning ring, (3 dc, ch 2) 2 times in ring, 3 dc in same ring, ch 1, (3 dc, ch 1) in end of each fp row across; working in 7-dc group on last row, 2 dc around post of next st, dc around post of next st, ch 2, dc around post of each of next 3 sts, ch 2, dc around post of next st, 2 dc around post of last st, ch 1, join with sl st in top of ch-3, fasten off.

Rnd 151: Join jade with sl st in first ch-1 sp, (ch 3, 2 dc) in same sp, *3 dc in each ch-1 sp around to next ch-2 sp, ch 1, (5 dc, ch 1) in each of next 2 ch-2 sps; repeat from *, 3 dc in last ch sp, join, fasten off.

ASSEMBLY

To **join Strips,** holding last Strip and this Strip wrong sides together, matching sts, working through both thicknesses in **back lps,** join jade with sc in 9th dc from center ch sp at one end, sc in each st across to last 3-dc group, fasten off.

Repeat with remaining Strips.

BORDER

Working around entire outer edge, skipping seams, join jade with sc in any st, sc in each st and 2 sc in each ch sp around, join with sl st in first sc, fasten off.

Peaches 'n Cream

Finished Size: 43" x 55"

Materials: Worsted-weight yarn — 38 oz. peach, 4 oz. white; G crochet hook or size needed to obtain gauge.

Gauge: 4 dc = 1"; 2 dc rows = 1".

Skill Level: ✧✧ Average

AFGHAN

Note: For **puff stitch (ps),** yo, insert hook in next ch or st, yo, draw up long lp, (yo, insert hook in same ch or st, yo, draw up long lp) 2 times, yo, draw through all 7 lps on hook.

Row 1: With peach, ch 247, dc in 4th ch from hook, ch 1, ps in next ch, ch 1, dc in each of next 2 chs, (skip next 10 chs, dc in each of next 2 chs, ch 1, ps in next ch, ch 1, dc in each of next 2 chs) across, turn. Back of row 1 is right side of work.

Rows 2-87: Ch 3, dc in next st, ch 1, ps in next ps, ch 1, dc in each of next 2 sts, (ch 10, skip next ch-10 sp, dc in each of next 2 sts, ch 1, ps in next ps, ch 1, dc in each of next 2 sts) across, turn.

Note: For **cable loops,** with right side of work facing you, starting at first skipped ch-10 lp on starting ch, working vertically across ch-10 lps to last row, fold first ch-10 lp left to right forming a lp *(see illustration No. 1)*. With crochet hook, draw next ch-10 lp through, twisting left over right *(see illustration No. 2)*. Continue working in this manner across to last

row. Repeat on each section of ch-10 lps.

Row 88: Ch 3, dc in next st, ch 1, ps in next ps, ch 1, dc in each of next 2 sts, (ch 1, sc in next twisted ch-10 lp, ch 1, dc in each of next 2 sts, ch 1, ps in next ps, ch 1, dc in each of next 2 sts) across, fasten off.

EDGING

Notes: For **picot,** ch 4, sc in 2nd ch from hook.

For **shell,** (2 dc, picot, 2 dc) in next ch sp.

Join white with sl st in first ps on last row of Afghan, (ch 3, dc, picot, 2 dc) in same ps, (ch 3, sc in next ch-1 sp before cable loop, sc in next ch-1 sp after cable loop, ch 3, shell in next ps) 16 times, (ch 3, skip next row, sc in end of next row) across, ch 3; working in starting ch on opposite side of row 1, shell in base of next ps, (ch 3, sc in next ch-10 sp before cable loop, sc in same ch sp after cable loop, ch 3, shell in base of next ps) 16 times, (ch 3, skip next row, sc in next row, across, ch 3, join with sl st in top of beginning ch-3, fasten off.

CABLE LOOP

No. 1

No. 2

Country Spice

Finished Size: 47½" x 61½"
not including Tassels

Materials: Worsted-weight yarn — 19 oz. jeweltone
variegated, 18 oz. off-white, 11 oz. blue, 10 oz. rose;
tapestry needle; H crochet hook or size needed to obtain gauge.

Gauge: 7 sts = 2"; rnds 1-5 = 4" across; Each Motif is 7" square.

Skill Level: ◇◇ Average

MOTIF (make 48)

Rnd 1: With variegated, ch 4, sl st in first ch to form ring, ch 1, 8 sc in ring, join with sl st in first sc (8 sc).

Rnd 2: Working this rnd in **front lps** only, ch 2, (dc, ch 2, sl st) in first st, (sl st, ch 2, dc, ch 2, sl st) in each st around, join with sl st in joining sl st of last rnd, fasten off.

Rnd 3: Working this rnd in **back lps** of rnd 1, join blue with sc in first st, sc in same st, 2 sc in each st around, join with sl st in first sc (16 sc).

Rnd 4: Ch 1, sc in first st, ch 3, skip next st, (sc in next st, ch 3, skip next st) around, join (8 sc, 8 ch sps).

Rnd 5: Sl st in first ch sp, ch 3, (2 dc, ch 2, 3 dc) in same sp, ch 2, skip next ch sp, *(3 dc, ch 2, 3 dc) in next ch sp, ch 2, skip next ch sp; repeat from * around, join with sl st in top of ch-3, fasten off (24 dc, 8 ch-2 sps).

Note: For **long sc (lsc),** working over ch sp on last rnd, insert hook in ch sp on rnd before last, yo, draw up long lp, yo, draw through both lps on hook.

Rnd 6: Join rose with sc in any corner ch sp, (sc, ch 2, 2 sc) in same sp, *skip next st, sc in each of next 2 sts, 3 lsc in next ch sp on rnd before last, sc in each of next 2 sts, skip next st, (2 sc, ch 2, 2 sc) in next corner ch-2 sp; repeat from * 2 more times, skip next st, sc in each of next 2 sts, 3 lsc in next ch sp on rnd before last, sc in each of next 2 sts, skip next st, join with

sl st in first sc, fasten off (44 sts, 4 ch-2 sps).

Rnd 7: Join off-white with sc in any corner ch sp, ch 2, sc in same sp, sc in each st around with (sc, ch 2, sc) in each corner ch sp, join, fasten off (52 sc, 4 ch-2 sps).

Rnd 8: Join variegated with sl st in any corner ch sp, ch 4, dc in same sp, *[skip next st, dc in next st, ch 1; working around last dc made, dc in same corner ch sp as dc before last, (skip next st, dc in next st, ch 1; working around last dc made, dc in last worked st) across to one st before next corner ch sp, skip next st, dc in next corner ch sp, ch 1; working around last st made, dc in last worked st], (dc, ch 1, dc) in same corner ch sp; repeat from * 2 more times; repeat between [ ], join with sl st in 3rd ch of ch-4, fasten off (32 ch-1 sps).

Rnd 9: Join off-white with sc in any corner ch sp, (sc, ch 2, 2 sc) in same sp, 2 sc in each ch-1 sp around with (2 sc, ch 2, 2 sc) in each corner ch-1 sp, join with sl st in first sc (72 sc).

Rnd 10: Ch 1, sc in each st around with (sc, ch 2, sc) in each corner ch sp, join, fasten off (80 sc).

ASSEMBLY

Holding Motifs wrong sides together, matching sts, with off-white, working through **back lps** only, sew Motifs together, making six rows of eight Motifs each.

Continued on page 76

Country Spice

Continued from page 75

BORDER

Rnd 1: Join off-white with sc in any corner ch sp, ch 2, sc in same sp, sc in next 20 sts, *[(dc next ch sps before and after seam tog, sc in next 20 sts) across to next corner], (sc, ch 2, sc) in next corner ch sp; repeat from * 2 more times; repeat between [ ], join with sl st in first sc, fasten off (169 sts on each long edge, 127 sts on each each short end, 4 corner ch sps).

Rnd 2: Join blue with sc in any corner ch sp, ch 2, sc in same sp, [*ch 1, skip next st, (sc in next st, ch 1, skip next st) across to next corner], (sc, ch 2, sc) in next corner ch sp; repeat from * 2 more times; repeat between [ ], join, fasten off (171 chs and sts on each long edge, 129 chs and sts on each short end, 4 ch-2 sps).

Rnd 3: Join rose with sc in any corner ch sp, ch 2, sc in same sp, *(ch 1, sc in next ch-1 sp) across to next corner, ch 1, (sc, ch 2, sc) in next corner ch sp; repeat from * 2 more times; (ch 1, sc in next ch-1 sp) across to next corner, ch 1, join, fasten off (173 chs and sts on each long edge, 131 chs and sts on each short end, 4 ch-2 sps).

Rnd 4: Join off-white with sc in any corner ch sp, (sc, ch 2, 2 sc) in same sp, *3 sc in next ch sp, 2 sc in each ch sp across to next corner, (2 sc, ch 2, 2 sc) in next corner ch sp; repeat from * 2 more times, 3 sc in next ch sp, 2 sc in each ch sp across to next corner, join, fasten off (177 sc on each long edge, 135 on each short end, 4 corner ch sps).

Rnd 5: Join variegated with sl st in any corner ch sp, ch 4, dc in same sp, *[skip next st, dc in next st, ch 1; working around last dc made, dc in same corner ch sp as dc before last, (skip next st, dc in next st, ch 1; working around last dc made, dc in last worked st) across to one st before next corner ch sp, skip next st, dc in next corner ch sp, ch 1; working around last st made, dc in last worked st], (dc, ch 1, dc) in same corner ch sp; repeat from * 2 more times; repeat between [ ], join with sl st in 3rd ch of ch-4, fasten off (318 ch-1 sps).

Rnd 6: Join off-white with sc in corner ch sp before one short end, (sc, ch 2, 2 sc) in same sp, 2 sc in each ch-1 sp around with (2 sc, ch 2, 2 sc) in each corner ch sp, join with sl st in first sc (182 sc on each long edge, 140 sc on each short end, 4 corner ch sps).

Rnd 7: Sl st in next st, sl st in next corner ch sp, ch 1, (sc, ch 1, hdc, dc) in same sp, [◊*skip next st, sl st in next st, (sc, ch 1, hdc, dc) in next st; repeat from * across to 2 sts before next corner ch sp, skip next st◊, sl st in next st, (sc, ch 1, hdc, dc) in next corner ch sp]; repeat between [ ] 2 more times; repeat between ◊◊, sl st in same st as first sl st, join, fasten off.

Raspberry Sherbet

Continued from page 66

Row 50: Join black with sl st in first st, ch 3, 2 dc in same st, (dc in next 5 sts, dc next 5 sts tog, dc in next 5 sts, 5 dc in next st, dc in next 10 sts, dc next 5 sts tog, dc in next 10 sts, 5 dc in next st) 3 times, dc in next 5 sts, dc next 5 sts tog, dc in next 5 sts, 3 dc in last st, turn, fasten off.

Row 51: Join white with sl st in first st, ch 3, 2 dc in same st, (dc in next 5 sts, dc next 5 sts tog, dc in next 5 sts, 5 dc in next st, dc in next 10 sts, dc next 5 sts tog, dc in next 10 sts, 5 dc in next st) 3 times, dc in next 5 sts, dc next 5 sts tog, dc in next 5 sts, 3 dc in last st, turn, fasten off.

Row 52: Repeat row 50.

Row 53: Join rose with sl st in first st, ch 3, 2 dc in same st, (dc in next 5 sts, dc next 5 sts tog, dc in next 5 sts, 5 dc in next st, dc in next 10 sts, dc next 5 sts tog, dc in next 10 sts, 5 dc in next st) 3 times, dc in next 5 sts, dc next 5 sts tog, dc in next 5 sts, 3 dc in last st, turn, fasten off.

Row 54: Repeat row 50.

Row 55: Join white with sl st in first st, ch 3, 2 dc in same st, (dc in next 5 sts, dc next 5 sts tog, dc in next 5 sts, 5 dc in next st, dc in next 10 sts, dc next 5 sts tog, dc in next 10 sts, 5 dc in next st) 3 times, dc in next 5 sts, dc next 5 sts tog, dc in next 5 sts, 3 dc in last st, turn, fasten off.

Row 56: Repeat row 50.

Row 57: Join rose with sl st in first st, ch 3, 2 dc in same st, (dc in next 5 sts, dc next 5 sts tog, dc in next 5 sts, 5 dc in next st, dc in next 10 sts, dc next 5 sts tog, dc in next 10 sts, 5 dc in next st) 3 times, dc in next 5 sts, dc next 5 sts tog, dc in next 5 sts, 3 dc in last st, turn, **do not** fasten off.

Rows 58-63: Ch 3, 2 dc in same st, (dc in next 5 sts, dc next 5 sts tog, dc in next 5 sts, 5 dc in next st, dc in next 10 sts, dc next 5 sts tog, dc in next 10 sts, 5 dc in next st) 3 times, dc in next 5 sts, dc next 5 sts tog, dc in next 5 sts, 3 dc in last st, turn. At end of last row, **do not** turn, fasten off.

Row 64: Join black with sc in first st, sc in each st across skipping one st at each valley and placing 3 sts at each peak, **do not** turn, fasten off.

Row 65: Join white with sc in first st, sc in each st across skipping one st at each valley and placing 3 sts at each peak, **do not** turn, fasten off.

Row 66: Join rose with sl st in first st, (ch 1, sl st in next st) across, fasten off.

Row 67: Working in starting ch on opposite side of row 1, join black with sc in first ch, sc in each ch across skipping one ch at each valley and placing 3 sts at each peak, **do not** turn, fasten off.

Row 68: Join white with sc in first st, sc in each st across skipping one st at each valley and placing 3 sts at each peak, **do not** turn, fasten off.

Row 69: Join rose with sl st in first st, (ch 1, sl st in next st) across, fasten off.

FRINGE

For **each Fringe,** cut 13 strands rose each 18" long. With all strands held together, fold in half, insert hook in ch sp, draw fold through sp, draw all loose ends through fold, tighten. Trim ends.

Fringe in ch sp at each peak and each valley on each short end of Afghan as shown in photo.

Immerse yourself in the splendors
of flowers and lace with this exquisite
marriage of innocent blossoms and delicate
designs. Relish the radiance of vivid whites
and tantalizing florals in an exhilarating
union inspired by love's mystical spell.
This passionate display of embraceable
afghans is destined to set hearts ablaze in
the eternal quest for romance and beauty.

Romantic Allure

Love in Bloom

Finished Size: 50" x 69"

Materials: Worsted-weight yarn — 42 oz. off-white,
19 oz. green and 17 oz. rose; tapestry needle;
G crochet hook or size needed to obtain gauge.

Gauge: 4 dc = 1"; 2 dc rnds = 1".
Each Motif is 9½" square.

Skill Level: ✧✧ Average

FLOWER MOTIF (make 18)
Center

Rnd 1: With rose, ch 2, 8 sc in 2nd ch from hook, join with sl st in first sc (8 sc).

Rnd 2: (Ch 4, sl st in next st) 7 times, ch 2, join with hdc in joining sl st on last rnd (8 ch sps).

Rnd 3: (*Ch 7, sl st in next ch sp, ch 9*, sl st in next ch sp) 3 times; repeat between **, join with sl st in joining sl st on last rnd, fasten off (4 ch-9 sps, 4 ch-7 sps).

For **leaves,** join green with sl st in 5th ch of any ch-9 sp on Center, (ch 3, tr, ch 3, sl st, ch 4, dtr, ch 4, sl st, ch 3, tr, ch 3, sl st) in same ch, fasten off.

Repeat on last three ch-9 sps.

Background

Rnd 1: With off-white, ch 4, sl st in first ch to form ring, ch 3, 2 dc in ring, ch 3, (3 dc in ring, ch 3) 3 times, join with sl st in top of ch-3 (12 dc, 4 ch sps).

Rnd 2: Ch 3, dc in each st around with (2 dc, ch 3, 2 dc) in each ch sp, join (28 dc, 4 ch sps).

Rnd 3: Ch 1, sc in first st; holding wrong side of Center to right side of Background Motif, with leaves at corners, *[sc in 4th ch of next ch-7 sp on Center and in next st on Background at same time; working behind leaves, sc in each of next 3 sts on Background, (2 sc, ch 3, 2 sc) in next ch sp], sc in each of next 3 sts; repeat from * 2 more times; repeat between [ ], sc in each of last 2 sts, join with sl

st in first sc (44 sc, 4 ch sps).

Rnd 4: Sl st in next st, ch 4, skip next st, *(dc in next st, ch 1, skip next st) across to next corner ch sp, (dc, ch 3, dc) in next ch sp, ch 1, skip next st; repeat from * 3 times, (dc in next st, ch 1, skip next st) 2 times, join with sl st in 3rd ch of ch-4 (28 dc, 24 ch-1 sps, 4 ch-3 sps).

Rnd 5: Ch 1, sc in first st, sc in next ch sp, sc in next st; *[to join leaves, sc in first tr on next leaf and in next ch sp on Background at same time, (sc in next st on Background, sc in next ch sp) 2 times, (sc, ch 1, sc) in dtr on leaf and in same ch sp on Background at same time, sc in same ch sp on Background, sc in next st, sc in next ch sp, sc in next st, sc in next tr on leaf and in next ch sp on Background at same time], sc in next 5 sts and ch sps on Background; repeat from * 2 more times; repeat between [ ], sc in next st, sc in last ch sp, join (68 sc, 4 ch-1 sps).

Rnd 6: Ch 3, dc in each st around with (dc, ch 3, dc) in each corner ch sp, join with sl st in top of ch-3 (76 dc, 4 ch sps).

Rnd 7: Ch 1, sc in each st around with (2 sc, ch 2, 2 sc) in each corner ch sp, join with sl st in first sc, fasten off (92 sc, 4 ch sps).

Notes: For **beginning cluster (beg cl),** ch 3, (yo, insert hook in same st or sp, yo, draw lp through, yo, draw through 2 lps on hook) 2 times, yo, draw through all 3 lps on hook.

For **cluster (cl),** yo, insert hook in next st or ch sp, yo, draw lp through, yo, draw through 2

Continued on page 94

Floral Infatuation

Finished Size: 55" x 73"

Materials: Worsted-weight yarn — 38 oz. white, 7 oz. rose and 5 oz. teal; tapestry needle; I crochet hook or size needed to obtain gauge.

Gauge: Rnd 1 of Motif = 1¼" across; cluster =1" tall.

Skill Level: ✧✧ Average

FIRST ROW
First Motif

Rnd 1: With rose, ch 5, sl st in first ch to form ring, ch 1, (sc in ring, ch 3) 8 times, join with sl st in first sc (8 sc, 8 ch lps).

Rnd 2: Sl st in first ch lp, ch 1, (sc, ch 1, dc, ch 1, dc, ch 1, dc, ch 1, sc) in same lp and in each ch lp around, join (40 sts, 32 ch sps).

Rnd 3: Sl st in first ch sp, ch 1, sc in same sp, (ch 4, sc in next ch sp) 3 times, *sc in next ch sp, (ch 4, sc in next ch sp) 3 times; repeat from * around, join (24 ch lps).

Rnd 4: Working behind last rnd, ch 5, skip next 3 ch lps, (sl st around post of next sc between petals, ch 5, skip next 3 ch lps) around, join with sl st in joining sl st on last rnd, fasten off (8 ch lps).

Notes: For **beginning cluster (beg cl),** ch 3, (yo, insert hook, yo, draw lp through, yo, draw through 2 lps on hook) 2 times in same ch sp, yo, draw through all 3 lps on hook.

For **cluster (cl),** (yo, insert hook, yo, draw lp through, yo, draw through 2 lps on hook) 3 times in next ch sp, yo, draw through all 4 lps on hook.

For **picot,** ch 3, sl st in top of sc just made.

Rnd 5: Join teal with sl st in any ch lp, (beg cl, ch 5, cl) in same lp, *[ch 5, (sc, picot, ch 3, sc, picot) in next ch lp, ch 5], (cl, ch 5, cl) in next ch lp; repeat from * 2 more times; repeat between [ ], join with sl st in top of beg cl, fasten off (16 ch lps).

Rnd 6: Join white with sl st in any ch lp between cls, (beg cl, ch 5, cl) in same lp, ch 5, (sc in next ch lp, picot, ch 5) 3 times, *(cl, ch 5, cl) in next ch lp, ch 5, (sc in next ch lp, picot, ch 5) 3 times; repeat from * around, join (20 ch lps).

Rnd 7: Sl st in first ch lp, (beg cl, ch 5, cl) in same lp, ch 5, (sc in next ch lp, picot, ch 5) 4 times, *(cl, ch 5, cl) in next ch lp, ch 5, (sc in next ch lp, picot, ch 5) 4 times; repeat from * around, join (24 ch lps).

Rnd 8: Sl st in first ch lp, (beg cl, ch 5, cl) in same lp, ch 5, (sc in next ch lp, ch 5) 5 times, *(cl, ch 5, cl) in next ch lp, ch 5, (sc in next ch lp, ch 5) 5 times; repeat from * around, join, fasten off (28 ch lps).

Second Motif

Rnds 1-7: Repeat same rnds of First Motif.

Notes: For **joining ch lp,** ch 2, sl st in center ch of corresponding ch lp on other Motif, ch 2.

Rnd 8: Sl st in first ch lp, (beg cl, ch 5, cl) in same lp, ch 5, (sc in next ch lp, ch 5) 5 times; to join to last Motif made, cl in next ch lp, work joining ch lp, cl in same ch sp on this Motif, work joining ch lp, (sc in next ch lp on this Motif, ch 5) 5 times, cl in next ch lp on this Motif, work joining ch lp, cl in same ch lp on this Motif, ch 5, (sc in next ch lp, ch 5) 5 times, (cl, ch 5, cl) in next ch lp, ch 5, (sc in

Continued on page 95

Midnight Meadows

Finished Size: 52" x 67"

Materials: Worsted-weight yarn — 25 oz. black,
14½ oz. each off-white and rose, 7 oz. each raspberry, teal and
sage green; F crochet hook or size needed to obtain gauge.

Gauge: 4 dc sts = 1". Each Motif is 7½" square.

Skill Level: ✧✧ Average

FIRST ROW
First Motif

Rnd 1: With sage, ch 6, sl st in first ch to form ring, ch 6, (dc in ring, ch 3) 7 times, join with sl st in 3rd ch of ch-6 (8 dc, 8 ch-3 sps).

Rnd 2: Sl st in first ch sp, ch 1; for **petals,** (sc, hdc, 3 dc, hdc, sc) in same sp and in each ch sp around, join with sl st in first sc (8 petals).

Note: For **front post stitch (fp,** *see fig. 14, page 158),* yo, insert hook from front to back around post of next st on rnd before last, yo, draw lp through, (yo, draw through 2 lps on hook) 2 times.

Rnd 3: Working behind petals, ch 1, fp around first dc on rnd 1, ch 4, (fp around next dc on rnd 1, ch 4) around, join with sl st in first fp (8 fp, 8 ch-4 sps).

Rnd 4: Sl st in first ch sp, ch 1, (sc, hdc, 4 dc, hdc, sc) in same sp and in each ch sp around, join with sl st in first sc (8 petals).

Rnd 5: Working behind petals, ch 1, fp around first fp on rnd 3, ch 5, (fp around next fp on rnd 3, ch 5) around, join with sl st in first fp (8 fp, 8 ch-5 sps).

Rnd 6: Sl st in first ch sp, ch 1, (sc, hdc, 5 dc, hdc, sc) in same sp and in each ch sp around, join with sl st in first sc, fasten off (8 petals).

Notes: For **beginning shell (beg shell),** ch 3, (2 dc, ch 2, 3 dc) in same st or sp.

For **shell,** (3 dc, ch 2, 3 dc) in next st or ch sp.

Rnd 7: Skip first 4 sts on first petal, join off-white with sl st in next st, beg shell, (*ch 5, skip next 7 sts, sc in each of next 3 sts, ch 5, skip next 7 sts*, shell in next st) 3 times; repeat between **, join (12 sc, 8 ch-5 sps, 4 shells).

Rnd 8: Sl st in next 2 sts, sl st in next ch sp, beg shell, (*5 dc in next ch sp, skip next st, 3 dc in next st, 5 dc in next ch sp*, shell in ch sp of next shell) 3 times; repeat between **, join, fasten off (8 5-dc groups, 4 3-dc groups, 4 shells).

Rnd 9: Join black with sl st in ch sp of any shell, beg shell, (*3 dc in sp between same shell and next 5-dc group, 3 dc in center dc of same 5-dc group, 3 dc in sp between same 5-dc group and next 3-dc group, 3 dc in sp between same 3-dc group and next 5-dc group, 3 dc in center dc of same 5-dc group, 3 dc in sp between same 5-dc group and next shell*, shell in ch sp of next shell) 3 times; repeat between **, join (72 dc, 4 shells).

Rnd 10: Ch 1, sc in first st, ch 4, skip next st, sc in next st, ch 7, skip next ch sp, *(sc in next st, ch 4, skip next st, sc in next st) 8 times, ch 7, skip next ch sp; repeat from * 2 times; repeat between ( ) 7 times, join with sl st in first sc, fasten off (64 sc, 32 ch-4 sps, 4 ch-7 sps).

Second Motif

Rnds 1-6: Using color indicated on Assembly Diagram, repeat same rnds of First Motif.

Rnds 7-9: Repeat same rnds of First Motif.

Continued on page 96

Heather Trellis

Finished Size: 52" x 64"

Materials: Worsted-weight yarn — 27 oz. rose/blue/off-white variegated, 15½ oz. off-white and 12 oz. rose; I and J crochet hooks or sizes needed to obtain gauges.

Gauge: I hook, 1 shell and 2 dc sts = 2¼"; 11 shell rows = 8". J hook, 11 sts = 4".

Skill Level: ✧ Easy

STRIP (make 13)

Notes: For **beginning shell (beg shell),** ch 3, (2 dc, ch 2, 3 dc) in same sp.

For **shell,** (3 dc, ch 2, 3 dc) in next ch sp.

Rnd 1: With I hook and variegated, ch 4, sl st in first ch to form ring, beg shell in ring, ch 3, shell in ring; to **join,** dc in top of ch-3, turn (2 shells, 2 dc).

Row 2: Working in rows, ch 3, shell in ch sp of next shell, dc in top of next ch-3 leaving remaining shell unworked, **turn** (2 dc, 1 shell).

Rows 3-81: Ch 3, shell in next shell, dc in top of last ch-3, turn. At end of last row, **do not** turn, fasten off.

Note: Use J hook for remainder of pattern.

Rnd 82: Working around outer edge, join off-white with sl st in top of ch-3 on last row, ch 3, 2 dc in same st, sc in next shell, skip next 2 dc of same shell, 3 dc in next dc, ch 3; working in ends of rows, dc in top of same row, (dc around post of st on same row, dc in top of next row) across to rnd 1, dc in top of joining dc, dc around post of same st, (dc, ch 3, 3 dc) in same st as joining dc, sc in next ch sp, skip next 2 sts of shell, (3 dc, ch 3, dc) in next st, dc in next ch-3 sp, dc in top of same ch-3, (dc around post of last st on next row, dc in top of same row) across to last row, dc around ch-3 on last row, dc in top of same ch-3, ch 3, join with sl st in top of beginning ch-3, fasten off.

Rnd 83: Join rose with sc in any st, sc in each st around with 5 sc in each ch sp, join with sl st in first sc, fasten off.

Working in **back lps** and matching sts, sew long sides of Strips together from center corner st to center corner st.

BORDER

Rnd 1: Working around entire outer edge of afghan, join rose with sc in 3rd st of 5-sc corner before either short edge, 2 sc in same st, *sc in next 10 sts, (hdc in next st, dc in next seam, hdc in next st on next Strip, sc in next 9 sts) 12 times, sc in next st, 3 sc in next st, sc in each st across long edge to next center corner st*, 3 sc in next center corner st; repeat between **, join.

Rnd 2: Ch 3, dc in each st around with 3 dc in 2nd st of each 3-sc corner, join with sl st in top of ch-3, fasten off.

Rnd 3: Join off-white with sc in any corner, ch 2, sc in same st, ch 1, skip next st, (sc in next st, ch 1, skip next st) around to next corner, *(sc, ch 2, sc) in same corner, ch 1, skip next st, (sc in next st, ch 1, skip next st) around to next corner; repeat from * around, join with sl st in first sc.

Rnd 4: Ch 1, sc in each st and in each ch sp around with 3 sc in each corner, join, fasten off.

Wedded Bliss

Finished Size: 52" x 66"
when blocked

Materials: 3-ply sport yarn — 36 oz. white;
H crochet hook or size needed to obtain gauge.

Gauge: 7 dc sts = 2"; 5 dc rows = 2¾"

Skill Level: ✧✧ Average

SQUARE (make 12)

Rnd 1: Ch 6, sl st in first ch to form ring, ch 3, 23 dc in ring, join with sl st in top of ch-3 (24 dc).

Rnd 2: Sl st in next st, ch 3, 2 dc in same st, (ch 2, skip next 2 sts, 3 dc in next st) 7 times, ch 2, skip last st, join (24 dc, 8 ch sps).

Rnd 3: Ch 1, sc in first st, ch 2, (sc in next st, ch 2) 2 times, *sc in next ch sp, ch 2, (sc in next st, ch 2) 3 times; repeat from * around to last ch sp, sc in last ch sp, ch 2, join with sl st in first sc (32 ch sps).

Rnd 4: Sl st in first ch sp, ch 1, sc in same sp, ch 2, (sc in next ch sp, ch 2) around, join.

Rnd 5: Sl st in first ch sp, ch 1, sc in same sp, *(3 hdc in next ch sp, 3 dc in next ch sp, 5 tr in next ch sp, 3 dc in next ch sp, 3 hdc in next ch sp), sc in each of next 3 ch sps; repeat from * 2 more times; repeat between ( ), sc in each of last 2 ch sps, join (80 sts).

Note: For **cluster (cl),** (yo, insert hook in st, yo, draw lp through, yo, draw through 2 lps on hook) 5 times in next st, yo, draw through all 6 lps on hook.

For **beginning cluster (beg cl),** ch 3, (yo, insert hook in st, yo, draw lp through, yo, draw through 2 lps on hook) 4 times in same st, yo, draw through all 5 lps on hook.

Rnd 6: Sl st in next st, ch 3, dc in next 6 sts, *[ch 1, (dc in next st, ch 1) 3 times, dc in next 7 sts, skip next st, cl in next st, skip next st], dc in next 7 sts; repeat from * 2 more times;

repeat between [ ], join with sl st in top of ch-3 (68 dc, 16 ch-1 sps, 4 cls).

Rnd 7: Beg cl, *[skip next dc, dc in next 5 dc, 2 dc in next ch sp, (ch 1, 2 dc in next ch sp) 3 times, dc in next 5 dc, skip next dc, cl in next dc, cl in top of next cl], cl in next dc; repeat from * 2 more times; repeat between [ ], join with sl st in top of beg cl (72 dc, 12 cls, 12 ch-1 sps).

Rnd 8: Ch 3, *[dc in next 7 dc, 2 dc in next ch-1 sp, ch 1, 3 dc in next ch-1 sp, ch 1, 2 dc in next ch-1 sp, dc in next 7 dc], dc in each of next 3 cls; repeat from * 2 more times; repeat between [ ], dc in each of last 2 cls, join with sl st in top of ch-3 (96 dc, 8 ch-1 sps).

Rnd 9: Ch 3, dc in next 9 sts, *[2 dc in next ch sp, ch 1, skip next st, 3 dc in next st, ch 1, skip next st, 2 dc in next ch sp], dc in next 21 sts; repeat from * 2 more times; repeat between [ ], dc in last 11 sts, join (112 dc, 8 ch sps).

Rnd 10: Ch 4, skip next st, (dc in next st, ch 1, skip next st) 5 times, *[dc in next ch sp, ch 1, skip next st, (dc, ch 1, dc, ch 1, dc) in next st, ch 1, skip next st, dc in next ch sp, ch 1, skip next st], (dc in next st, ch 1, skip next st) 12 times; repeat from * 2 more times; repeat between [ ], (dc in next st, ch 1, skip next st) 6 times, join with sl st in 3rd ch of ch-4 (68 dc, 68 ch sps).

Note: For **beginning V-stitch (beg V-st),** ch 4, dc in same st or sp.

Continued on page 97

Lover's Lace

Finished Size: 48" x 72"

Materials: Worsted-weight yarn — 16 oz. each off-white and rose; No. 50 broomstick lace pin; H crochet hook or size needed to obtain gauge.

Gauge: 3 5-loop broomstick lace groups = 4"; broomstick portion of Panel = 3" wide. Entire Panel = 6" wide.

Skill Level: ✧✧ Average

FIRST PANEL

Row 1: With rose, ch 240, **do not** turn; slip lp from hook onto broomstick pin (*see illustration No. 1*), insert hook in 2nd ch from pin (through top lp only), yo, draw lp through and slip onto pin, (insert hook in next ch, yo, draw lp through and slip onto pin) across, **do not** turn (240 lps on pin); [insert hook under first 5 lps on pin, slide lps off pin (*see illustration No. 2*), yo, draw lp through, ch 1, 5 sc in same 5-lp group (*see illustration No. 3*), *insert hook under next 5 lps on pin, slide off pin, yo, draw lp through, yo, draw through both lps on hook (first sc made), 4 more sc in same 5-lp group; repeat from * across], fasten off.

Note: When working row 2, be careful to pick up only the bottom lp of the starting ch. If done correctly, you will have a single raised ridge down the center on each side of the Panel. A thick ridge on one side with none on the other means the wrong lp was used.

Row 2: With right side of row 1 facing you and opposite side of starting ch at top, working from left to right in opposite of starting ch and leaving a long tail, draw up a lp in first ch at left end (do not use a slip knot), place lp on pin, (insert hook in next ch, yo, draw lp through and slip onto pin) across, **do not** turn; repeat between [ ] in row 1; tie tails at beginning of rows 1 and 2 together to secure; **do not** turn.

Row 3: Working through last 2 lps on same 5-lp group, (hdc, 2 dc, tr) in lps, tr in end of starting ch; working in first 2 lps of next 5-lp group, (tr, 2 dc, hdc) in lps, sl st in next sc, fasten off.

Row 4: Working on opposite end of broomstick strip, join rose with sl st in last sc of row 1; repeat row 3.

Rnd 5: Join off-white with sl st in center sc of first 5-sc group on one long edge, *(ch 5, sl st in center st of next 5-sc group) across to end, ch 5, skip last 2 sc of same 5-sc group, sl st in next hdc, ch 5, skip next dc, sl st in next dc, ch 3, skip next tr, (dc, ch 3, dc) in next center tr, ch 3, skip next tr, sl st in next dc, ch 5, skip next dc, sl st in next hdc; repeat from *, ch 5,

Continued on page 95

BROOMSTICK LACE

No. 1

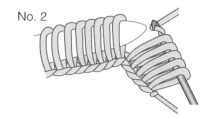

No. 2

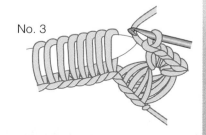

No. 3

Irresistible Charm

Finished Size: 50" x 58"
without fringe

Materials: Worsted-weight yarn — 25 oz. each coral
and white; H crochet hook or size needed to obtain gauge.

Gauge: 3 sts = 1"; 2 pattern rows = 1".

Skill Level: ✧✧ Average

AFGHAN

Note: At end of each row, **do not** turn. Work entire afghan with right side facing you.

Leave 8" strand of yarn at beginning and end of each row to form fringe.

Ch-3 at beginning of each row counts as first st.

Row 1: With coral, ch 149, fasten off.

Row 2: Join white with sc in first ch, sc in each ch across, fasten off (149 sc).

Row 3: Join coral with sl st in first st, ch 3, skip next st, (2 dc in next st, skip next st) across to last st, dc in last st, fasten off (148 dc).

Note: For **long dc (ldc),** working over last row, yo, insert hook in skipped st on row before last, yo, draw up long lp, complete as dc.

Row 4: Join white with sl st in first st, ch 3, skip next st, dc in sp between next 2 dc; (ldc in skipped st on row before last, dc in sp between next 2 dc) across to last st, dc in last st, fasten off.

Rows 5-14: Repeat rows 3 and 4 alternately.

Row 15: Join coral with sc in first st, sc in each st across, fasten off.

Rows 16-27: Reversing colors, repeat rows 3 and 4 alternately.

Row 28: Join white with sc in first st, sc in each st across, fasten off.

Rows 29-119: Repeat rows 3-28 consecutively, ending with row 15.

For **edging,** join coral with sc in end of row 1, spacing sts so edge lays flat, sc across ends of rows, fasten off.

Repeat on opposite side of afghan. Pull 8" strands at beginning and end of each row through nearest sc on edging.

For **each fringe,** cut 2 strands each color each 16" long. With all 4 strands held together, fold in half, insert hook in st, draw fold through, draw all loose ends through fold including yarn strands at ends of rows, tighten. Trim ends.

Fringe at end of every other row on short ends of afghan.🍂

Love in Bloom

Continued from page 81

lps on hook, (yo, insert hook in same st or sp, yo, draw lp through, yo, draw through 2 lps on hook; repeat from *, yo, draw through all 4 lps on hook.

Rnd 8: Join rose with sl st in any corner ch sp, beg cl, ch 4, cl in same sp, *[ch 2, skip next 2 sts, (cl in next st, ch 2, skip next 2 sts) 7 times], (cl, ch 4, cl) in next ch sp; repeat from * 2 more times; repeat between [ ], join with sl st in top of first cl, fasten off (36 cls, 32 ch-2 sps, 4 ch-4 sps).

Rnd 9: Join off-white with sc in any ch-2 sp, 2 sc in same sp, 3 sc in each ch-2 sp around with (2 sc, ch 3, 2 sc) in each corner ch-4 sp, join with sl st in first sc, fasten off (112 sc, 4 ch sps).

Rnd 10: Join green with sl st in first sc of first 3-sc group on one side, ch 2, skip next sc, dc in next sc, ch 2, *(dc first and last sc on next 3-sc group tog, ch 2) across to next 2-sc group at corner, dc first sc of 2-sc group and corner ch sp tog, ch 2, (dc, ch 2, dc) in same corner ch sp, ch 2, dc in same sp and 2nd st of next 2-sc group tog, ch 2; repeat from * 3 more times, join with sl st in top of first dc, fasten off (48 ch sps).

Rnd 11: Join off-white with sc in any ch sp on one side, 2 sc in same sp, 3 sc in each ch sp around with (2 sc, ch 1, 2 sc) in each corner ch sp, join with sl st in first sc, fasten off (148 sc, 4 ch sps).

PLAIN MOTIF (make 17)

Rnds 1-2: Repeat same rnds of Flower Motif Background.

Rnd 3: Ch 1, sc in each st around with (sc, ch 3, sc) in each corner ch sp, join with sl st in first sc (44 sc, 4 ch sps).

Rnd 4: Repeat same rnd of Flower Motif Background.

Rnd 5: Ch 1, sc in each st and in each ch sp around with (2 sc, ch 1, 2 sc) in each corner ch sp, join with sl st in first sc (68 sc, 4 ch sps).

Rnds 6-11: Repeat same rnds of Flower Motif Background.

Matching sts and corner ch-1 sps, starting with Flower Motif in upper left corner, alternating Motifs, with off-white, whipstitch Motifs together through **both lps** making five rows of seven Motifs each.

BORDER

Rnd 1: Join rose with sl st in first st of first 3-sc group on one long edge, ch 5, skip next 2 sts, dc in next st, [◊*(ch 2, skip next 2 sts, dc in next st) across to one st before next seam, ch 2, dc in seam, ch 2, skip next st, dc in next st, (ch 2, skip next 2 sts, dc in next st) across to 2 sts before next seam, ch 2, skip next 2 sts, dc in seam, ch 2, skip next 2 sts, dc in next st; repeat from * across to last Motif on this side, (ch 2, skip next 2 sts, dc in next st) across to one st before next corner ch sp, ch 2, skip next st, (dc, ch 2, dc) in next ch sp, ch 2, skip next 2 sts◊, dc in next st]; repeat between [ ] 2 more times; repeat between ◊◊, join with sl st in 3rd ch of ch-5, fasten off.

Notes: For **front cluster (front cl),** working in front of rnd 1, yo, insert hook in next skipped st on last rnd of Motif, yo, draw lp through, yo, draw through 2 lps on hook, skip next dc on rnd 1, yo, insert hook in next skipped st on Motif, yo, draw lp through, yo, draw through 2 lps on hook, yo, draw through all 3 lps on hook.

For **back cluster (back cl),** working behind rnd 1, yo, insert hook in next skipped st on last rnd of Motif, yo, draw lp through, yo, draw through 2 lps on hook, skip next dc on rnd 1, yo, insert hook in next skipped st on Motif, yo, draw lp through, yo, draw through 2 lps on hook, yo, draw through all 3 lps on hook.

For **front cluster variation (front cl-var),** working first half of st in **same** st as last half of previous st, work same as front cl.

For **back cluster variation (back cl-var),** working first half of st in **same** st as last half of previous st, work same as back cl.

Rnd 2: Join green with sl st in first skipped st on last rnd of Motifs before joining ch-5 on rnd 1, ch 2; working behind next dc on rnd 1, dc in skipped st after ch-5, ch 2, front cl, ch 2, (back cl, ch 2, front cl, ch 2) 5 times, [*back cl-var, front cl-var, (back cl, ch 2, front cl, ch 2) 12 times; repeat from * 2 more times; working behind sts of rnd 1 at corner, dc in same st as last half of previous cl, ch 3, dc in first skipped st after corner, ch 2, (front cl, ch 2, back cl, ch

2) 6 times, ◊front cl-var, ch 2, back cl-var, ch 2, (front cl, ch 2, back cl, ch 2) 12 times; repeat from ◊; working in front of sts on rnd 1 at corner, dc in same st as last half of previous cl, ch 3, dc in first skipped st after corner, ch 2], (back cl, ch 2, front cl, ch 2) 6 times; repeat between [ ], join, fasten off.

Rnd 3: Working in ch sps of rnds 1 and 2 at same time, join off-white with sc in first ch sp after any corner, ch 3, sc in same sp, sc in next cl or dc at back, [*(sc, ch 3, sc) in next ch sp, sc in next cl or dc at back; repeat from * across to ch sp before next corner, (sc, ch 3, sc) in next ch sp, (sc, ch 3, sc, ch 5, sc, ch 3, sc) in next corner ch sp]; repeat between [ ] 3 times, join with sl st in first sc, fasten off.⸙

Floral Infatuation

Continued from page 82

next ch lp, ch 5) 5 times, join, fasten off.

Repeat Second Motif six more times for a total of eight Motifs.

SECOND ROW
First Motif

Rnds 1-7: Repeat same rnds of First Motif on page 82.

Rnd 8: Joining to bottom of First Motif on last Row made, work same as Second Motif of Second Row.

Second Motif

Rnds 1-7: Repeat same rnds of First Motif on page 82.

Rnd 8: Sl st in first ch lp, (beg cl, ch 5, cl) in same lp, ch 5, (sc in next ch lp, ch 5) 5 times; working across side of last Motif made, cl in next ch lp, *work joining ch lp, cl in same ch sp on this Motif, work joining ch lp, (sc in next ch lp on this Motif, ch 5) 5 times, cl in next ch lp on this Motif; working across bottom of next Motif on last Row, repeat from *, ch 5, cl in same ch lp on this Motif, ch 5, (sc in next ch lp, ch 5) 5 times, join, fasten off.

Repeat Second Motif six more times for a total of eight Motifs.

Repeat Second Row four more times for a total of six Rows.

EDGING

Working around entire outer edge of afghan, join white with sc in any ch lp, ch 5, sc in same lp, ch 5, *(sc, ch 5, sc) in next ch lp, ch 5; repeat from * around, join with sl st in first sc, fasten off.⸙

Lover's Lace

Continued from page 90

join with sl st in first sc.

Note: For **picot,** ch 3, sl st in top of last st made.

Rnd 6: Sl st in next ch sp, ch 1, (3 sc, ch 3, 3 sc) in same sp, *(3 sc, ch 3, 3 sc) in each ch sp across to last ch-5 sp, (2 sc, picot, sc, hdc) in next ch-5 sp, (2 dc, picot, 2 dc) in next ch-3 sp, (dc, 2 tr, picot, 2 tr, dc) in end ch-3 sp, (2 dc, picot, 2 dc) in next ch-3 sp, (hdc, sc, picot, 2 sc) in next ch-5 sp; repeat from *, join, fasten off.

NEXT PANEL (make 6)

Row 1-Rnd 5: Repeat same rows/rnd of First Panel.

Rnd 6: Sl st in next ch sp, ch 1, (3 sc, ch 3, 3 sc) in same sp, (3 sc, ch 3, 3 sc) in each ch sp across to last ch-5 sp, *(2 sc, picot, sc, hdc) in next ch-5 sp, (2 dc, picot, 2 dc) in next ch-3 sp, (dc, 2 tr, picot, 2 tr, dc) in end ch-3 sp, (2 dc, picot, 2 dc) in next ch-3 sp, (hdc, sc, picot, 2 sc) in next ch-5 sp*; to join Panels, holding this Panel and last Panel made wrong sides tog, (3 sc in next ch-5 sp on this Panel, ch 1, sl st in corresponding ch-3 sp on other Panel, ch 1, 3 sc in same ch-5 sp on this Panel) across to last ch-5 sp on this panel; repeat between **, join, fasten off.⸙

Midnight Meadows
Continued from page 85

Rnd 10: Ch 1, sc in first st, ch 4, skip next st, sc in next st, ch 7, skip next ch sp, *(sc in next st, ch 4, skip next st, sc in next st) 8 times*, ch 7, skip next ch sp; repeat between **; working across side of last Motif made, ch 3, sl st in corresponding ch-7 sp on last Motif, ch 3, (sc in next st on this Motif, ch 2, sl st in corresponding ch-4 sp on last Motif, ch 2, skip next st on this Motif, sc in next st) 8 times, ch 3, sl st in next ch-7 sp on last Motif, ch 3, (sc in next st on this Motif, ch 4, skip next st, sc in next st) 7 times, join with sl st in first sc, fasten off (64 sc, 36 ch sps).

Repeat Second Motif four more times for a total of six Motifs.

SECOND ROW
First Motif

Rnds 1-6: Using color indicated on Assembly Diagram, repeat same rnds of First Motif on First Row.

Rnds 7-9: Repeat same rnds of First Motif on First Row.

Rnd 10: Ch 1, sc in first st, ch 4, skip next st, sc in next st, ch 7, skip next ch sp, *(sc in next st, ch 4, skip next st, sc in next st) 8 times*; ch 7, skip next ch sp; repeat between **; working across bottom of first Motif on last Row made, ch 3, sl st in corresponding ch-7 sp on last Motif, ch 3, (sc in next st on this

Assembly Diagram

Motif, ch 2, sl st in corresponding ch-4 sp on last Motif, ch 2, skip next st on this Motif, sc in next st) 8 times, ch 3, sl st in next ch-7 sp on last Motif, ch 3, (sc in next st on this Motif, ch 4, skip next st, sc in next st) 7 times, join with sl st in first sc, fasten off (64 sc, 36 ch sps).

Second Motif

Rnds 1-6: Using color indicated on Assembly Diagram, repeat same rnds of First Motif on First Row.

Rnds 7-9: Repeat same rnds of First Motif on First Row.

Rnd 10: Ch 1, sc in first st, ch 4, skip next st, sc in next st, ch 7, skip next ch sp, (sc in next st, ch 4, skip next st, sc in next st) 8 times; working across bottom of next Motif on last Row made, ch 3, sl st in joining sl st of first ch-7 sp on other Motif, ch 3, (sc in next st on this Motif, ch 2, sl st in corresponding ch-4 sp on other Motif, ch 2, skip next st on this Motif, sc in next st) 8 times, ch 3, sl st in joining sl st between Motifs, ch 3; working across side of last Motif made, (sc in next st on this Motif, ch 2, sl st in corresponding ch-4 sp on last Motif, ch 2, skip next st on this Motif, sc in next st) 8 times, ch 3, sl st in next ch-7 sp on last Motif, ch 3, (sc in next st on this Motif, ch 4, skip next st, sc in next st) 7 times, join with sl st in first sc, fasten off (64 sc, 36 ch sps).

Repeat Second Motif four more times for a total of six Motifs.

Repeat Second Row six more times for a total of eight Rows.

BORDER

Rnd 1: Working around entire outer edge, join black with sl st in top left corner ch-7 sp, beg shell, 3 dc in each ch-4 sp and in each ch-3 sp on each side of joinings around with shell in each corner ch-7 sp, join with sl st in top of ch-3, fasten off (58 3-dc groups on each short end between corner shells, 78 3-dc groups on each long edge between corner shells).

Rnd 2: Join off-white with sl st in first ch sp, beg shell, 3 dc in sp between each 3-dc group around with shell in ch sp of each shell, join, fasten off (59 3-dc groups on each short end between corner shells, 79 3-dc groups on each long edge between corner shells, 4 shells).

Rnds 3-6: Using color sequence of rose, teal, raspberry and sage, repeat rnd 2, ending with 63 3-dc groups on each short end between corner shells, 83 3-dc groups on each long edge between corner shells and 4 shells.

Rnd 7: Join off-white with sl st in first corner ch sp, ch 3, 2 dc in same sp, dc in each st around with 3 dc in each corner ch sp, join, fasten off (195 dc on each short edge between corner 3-dc groups, 255 dc on each long edge between corner 3-dc groups, 4 3-dc groups).

Rnd 8: Join black with sl st in first st of first 3-dc group, ch 3, dc in same st, 2 dc in each of next 2 sts, dc in each st across to next corner 3-dc group, (2 dc in each of next 3 sts, dc in each st across to next corner 3-dc group) around, join, fasten off (924 dc).

Rnd 9: Sl st in next st, ch 1, sc in same st, (ch 3, skip next st, sc in next st) 2 times, *[(ch 5, skip next 2 sts, sc in next st) across to 6 corner sts], (ch 3, skip next st, sc in next st) 3 times; repeat from * 2 times; repeat between [ ], ch 3, skip last st, join with sl st in first sc, fasten off.❧

Wedded Bliss

Continued from page 89

For **V-stitch (V-st),** (dc, ch 1, dc) in next st or sp.

Rnd 11: Sl st in first ch sp, ch 4, (dc in next ch sp, ch 1) 6 times, *(V-st in next ch sp, ch 1) 2 times, (dc in next ch sp, ch 1) 15 times; repeat from * 2 more times, (V-st in next ch sp, ch 1) 2 times, (dc in next ch sp, ch 1) 8 times, join (60 dc, 68 ch sps, 8 V-sts).

Rnd 12: Sl st in first ch sp, ch 3, dc in same sp, 2 dc in each of next 7 ch sps, 3 dc in next ch sp, (2 dc in each of next 18 ch sps, 3 dc in next ch sp) 3 times, 2 dc in each of last 10 ch sps, join with sl st in top of ch-3 (156 dc).

Rnd 13: Sl st in next 2 sts, beg V-st, skip next 2 sts, (V-st in next st, skip next 2 sts) 4 times, *(dc, ch 1) 4 times in next st, dc in same st, skip next 2 sts, (V-st in next st, skip next 2 sts) 12 times; repeat from * 2 more times, (dc, ch 1) 4 times in next st, dc in same st, skip next 2 sts, (V-st in next st, skip next 2 sts) 7 times, join with sl st in 3rd ch of ch-4 (48 V-sts, 20 dc, 16 ch-1 sps).

Rnd 14: Sl st in ch sp of first V-st, beg V-st, V-st in next 6 V-sts and ch-1 sps, ch 1, (V-st in next 16 ch sps and V-sts, ch 1) 3 times, V-st in last 9 ch sps and V-sts, join (64 V-sts, 4 ch sps). Block each piece, if desired.

ASSEMBLY

To **join,** holding two Squares right side up,

join with sc in corner ch sp between V-sts on first Square, ch 1, sc in corner ch sp between V-sts on other Square, (ch 1, sc in ch sp of next V-st on first Square, ch 1, sc in ch sp of next V-st on other Square) across ending with sc in corner ch sp between V-sts on other Square, fasten off.

Join Squares in 3 rows of 4 Squares each. (When working across long strips, work joining in ch-1 sps of previous joining also.)

BORDER

Rnd 1: Working around entire outer edge of afghan, join with sc in any corner ch sp, ch 2, sc in same sp, ch 2, (sc in next V-st, ch sp or joining, ch 2) around with (sc, ch 2, sc, ch 2) in each corner ch sp, join with sl st in first sc (57 ch sps across each short end, 77 ch sps across each long edge).

Rnd 2: Sl st in first corner ch sp, ch 4, (dc, ch 1, dc, ch 1, dc, ch 1, dc) in same sp, [◊sc in next ch sp, *(dc, ch 1, dc, ch 1, dc) in next ch sp, sc in next ch sp; repeat from * across to next corner ch sp◊, dc in next corner ch sp, (ch 1, dc) 4 times in same sp]; repeat between [ ] 2 more times; repeat between ◊◊, join with sl st in 3rd ch of ch-4.

Rnd 3: Sl st in first ch sp, beg V-st, V-st in each ch sp and sc in each sc around, join, fasten off.❧

Cultivate an ever-lasting garden of
unparalleled beauty as a private
hideaway in which to surround yourself
with the peaceful calm of nature's purity.
Bursting forth in an effervescent
bouquet, these blue-ribbon hybrids let
you rejuvenate your decor with a
breath of eternal spring. Set your spirit
free as you wander through this
resplendent profusion of flowered stitchery.

Fragrant Flourishes

Morning Glory

Finished Size: 49" x 63"

Materials: Worsted-weight yarn — 29 oz. white and 11 oz. blue; I crochet hook or size needed to obtain gauge.

Gauge: Rnds 1-2 = 4" across. Each Motif is 7" across.

Skill Level: ✧✧ Average

FIRST ROW
First Motif

Rnd 1: With blue, ch 4, sl st in first ch to form ring, ch 1, (sc in ring, ch 2) 8 times, join with sl st in first sc (8 sc, 8 ch-2 sps).

Notes: For **beginning cluster (beg cl),** ch 4, *yo 2 times, insert hook in same sp, yo, draw lp through, (yo, draw through 2 lps on hook) 2 times; repeat from * 2 more times, yo, draw through all 4 lps on hook.

For **cluster (cl),** yo 2 times, insert hook in next ch sp, yo, draw lp through, (yo, draw through 2 lps on hook) 2 times, *yo 2 times, insert hook in same sp, yo, draw lp through, (yo, draw through 2 lps on hook) 2 times; repeat from * 2 more times, yo, draw through all 5 lps on hook.

Rnd 2: Sl st in first ch sp, beg cl, ch 4, (cl in next ch sp, ch 4) around, join with sl st in top of beg cl, fasten off (8 cls, 8 ch-4 sps).

Rnd 3: Join white with sl st in any ch sp, ch 3, 5 dc in same sp, 6 dc in each ch sp around, join with sl st in top of ch-3 (48 dc).

Rnd 4: Ch 5, skip next st, (dc in next st, ch 2, skip next st) around, join with sl st in 3rd ch of ch-5 (24 dc, 24 ch-2 sps).

Rnd 5: Sl st in first ch sp, ch 1, sc in same sp, ch 5, (sc in next ch sp, ch 5) around, join with sl st in first sc, fasten off (24 ch sps).

Second Motif

Rnds 1-4: Repeat same rnds of First Motif.
Note: For **joining ch sp,** ch 2, drop lp from

hook, insert hook in next ch sp on last Motif, pick up dropped lp, ch 3.

Rnd 5: Sl st in first ch sp, ch 1, sc in same sp, (ch 5, sc in next ch sp) 21 times; to join, working joining ch sp in 12th ch sp on last Motif made, (sc in next ch sp on this Motif, work joining ch sp in next ch sp on last Motif) 2 times, join with sl st in first sc, fasten off.

Repeat Second Motif four more times for a total of six Motifs.

SECOND ROW
First Motif

Rnds 1-4: Repeat same rnds of First Motif on First Row.

Rnd 5: Sl st in first ch sp, ch 1, sc in same sp, (ch 5, sc in next ch sp) 21 times; joining to bottom of First Motif on last Row made, work joining ch-5 sp in 6th ch sp on last Motif, (sc in next ch sp on this Motif, work joining ch sp in next ch sp on last Motif) 2 times, join with sl st in first sc, fasten off.

Second Motif

Rnds 1-4: Repeat same rnds of First Motif on First Row.

Rnd 5: Sl st in first ch sp, ch 1, sc in same sp, (ch 5, sc in next ch sp) 15 times; joining to bottom of next Motif on last Row made, work joining ch-5 sp in 6th ch sp on last Motif, (sc in next ch sp on this Motif, work joining ch sp in next

Continued on page 111

Floating Gardens

Finished Size: 53" x 63"

Materials: Worsted-weight yarn — 21 oz. lt. teal, 18 oz. dk. teal, 14 oz. dk. plum, 7 oz. lt. plum and 3½ oz. yellow; G crochet hook or size needed to obtain gauge.

Gauge: Rnd 1 of Motif = 1½" across. Each Motif = 10" square.

Skill Level: ✧✧ Average

MOTIF (make 30)

Note: Wrong side of stitches will be right side of work.

Rnd 1: With yellow, ch 4, sl st in first ch to form ring, ch 3, 15 dc in ring, join with sl st in top of ch-3 (16 dc).

Rnd 2: Working this rnd in **back lps** (*see fig. 1, page 156*), ch 1, sc in first st, ch 3, (sc in next st, ch 3) around, join with sl st in first sc, fasten off (16 ch lps).

Rnd 3: Working this rnd in **front lps** of rnd 1, join lt. plum with sl st in first st, ch 4, 6 tr in same st, skip next st, sc in next st, skip next st, (7 tr in next st, skip next st, sc in next st, skip next st) around, join with sl st in top of ch-4 (28 tr, 4 sc).

Rnd 4: Repeat rnd 2 (32 ch lps).

Rnd 5: Working this rnd in **front lps** of rnd 3, join dk. plum with sc in any sc, *(tr in each of next 2 tr, 2 tr in next tr, 3 tr in next tr, 2 tr in next tr, tr in each of next 2 tr), sc in next sc; repeat from * 2 more times; repeat between ( ), join with sl st in first sc (44 tr, 4 sc).

Rnd 6: Ch 1, sc in first sc, *(dc in each of next 2 tr, 2 dc in each of next 3 tr, 3 dc in next tr, 2 dc in each of next 3 tr, dc in each of next 2 tr), sc in next sc; repeat from * 2 more times; repeat between ( ), join (76 dc, 4 sc).

Rnd 7: Repeat rnd 2 (80 ch lps).

Note: For **beginning popcorn (beg pc),** ch 4, 6 tr in same st, drop lp from hook, insert hook in top of ch-4, draw dropped lp through lp on hook, ch 1. Push through to right side of work.

For **popcorn (pc),** 7 tr in next st, drop lp from hook, insert hook in top of first tr made, draw dropped lp through lp on hook, ch 1. Push through to right side of work.

Rnd 8: Working this rnd in **front lps** of rnd 6, join dk. teal with sl st in any sc, beg pc, *[skip next 2 sts, sc in next st, skip next 2 sts, 7 tr in next st, (skip next 3 sts, 7 tr in next st) 2 times, skip next 2 sts, sc in next st, skip next 2 sts], pc in next sc; repeat from * 2 more times; repeat between [ ], join with sl st in top of first pc (84 tr, 8 sc, 4 pc).

Rnd 9: Ch 1, sc in top of first pc, *(skip next sc, dc in next 10 tr, 3 dc in next tr, dc in next 10 tr, skip next sc), sc in top of next pc; repeat from * 2 more times; repeat between ( ), join with sl st in first sc (92 dc, 4 sc).

Rnd 10: Working this rnd in **back lps,** ch 1, sc in each dc and in each sc around with (sc, ch 3, sc) in center dc of each 3-dc group, join, fasten off.

Rnd 11: Working this rnd in **front lps** of rnd 9, join lt. teal with sl st in same st as joining, ch 4, 2 tr in same st, *(skip next st, dc in next 10 sts, 5 dc in next st, dc in next 10 sts, skip next st), 3 tr in next st; repeat from * 2 more times; repeat between ( ), join with sl st in top of ch-4 (100 dc, 12 tr).

Rnds 12-13: Ch 3, dc in each st around with 3 dc in each center corner st, join with sl st in

Continued on page 110

Lily of the Nile

Finished Size: 46½" x 63"

Materials: Worsted-weight yarn — 15 oz. dk. green, 12 oz. med. green, 5½ oz. lavender, 3 oz. lilac, 2½ oz. purple and 2 oz. each med. and dk. blue; G crochet hook or size needed to obtain gauge.

Gauge: 4 sc sts = 1"; Rnds 1-2 = 4" tip to tip; Motif = 5½" across.

Skill Level: ✧✧ Average

MOTIF (make 95, see note)

Note: Make 28 purple/lavender, 27 lavender/lilac, 20 med. blue/lilac and 20 dk. blue/lavender.

Rnd 1: With first flower color, ch 4, sl st in first ch to form ring, ch 1, (sc in ring, ch 10, sl st in last sc made) 6 times, join with sl st in first sc, fasten off (6 ch-10 lps).

Rnd 2: Join next flower color with sc in any sc, ch 4, (sc, ch 3, sc) in next ch-10 lp, ch 4, *sc in next sc, ch 4, (sc, ch 3, sc) in next ch-10 lp, ch 4; repeat from * around, join, fasten off.

Rnd 3: Join dk. green with sc in any ch-3 sp,

ASSEMBLY DIAGRAM ← Join

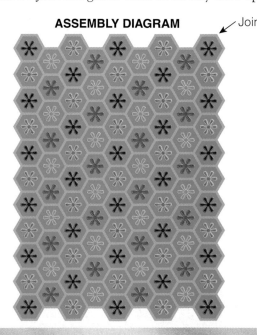

ch 2, sc in same sp, ch 2, tr in next sc between petals, ch 2, *(sc, ch 2, sc) in next ch-3 sp, ch 2, tr in next sc between petals, ch 2; repeat from * around, join (18 ch-2 sps, 12 sc, 6 tr).

Rnd 4: Ch 1, sc in first st, *(sc, ch 2, sc) in next ch-2 sp, sc in next st, (2 sc in next ch sp, sc in next st) 2 times; repeat from * 4 more times, (sc, ch 2, sc) in next ch-2 sp, (sc in next st, 2 sc in next ch sp) 2 times, join, fasten off (54 sc, 6 ch-2 sps).

Rnd 5: Join med. green with sc in any ch-2 sp, ch 2, sc in same sp, *[ch 1, skip next st, (sc in next st, ch 1, skip next st) across] to next ch-2 sp, (sc, ch 2, sc) in next ch-2 sp; repeat from * 4 more times; repeat between [ ], join, fasten off (36 sc, 30 ch-1 sps, 6 ch-2 sps).

With right sides up, matching sts and ch sps, with med. green, sew Motifs together through **back lps** only according to Assembly Diagram.

BORDER

Rnd 1: Working around entire outer edge, join med. green with sc in top right-hand corner ch-2 sp (see diagram), ch 2, sc in same sp, ch 1; skipping sc sts, (sc, ch 1) in each ch-1 sp and in each ch-2 sp before and after seams around with (sc, ch 2, sc, ch 1) in ch-2 sp on each outer point around, join with sl st in first sc.

Notes: Rnd 2 of Border is worked in four sections, parts A, B, C and D. When working each section, repeat only instructions from that section unless otherwise stated.

Continued on page 111

Floral Chambers

Finished Size: 52" x 72"

Materials: Worsted-weight yarn — 25 oz. off-white, 21 oz. pale green, 12 oz. dk. rose and 8 oz. lt rose; (optional) Glue 'n Wash for fabric; H crochet hook or size needed to obtain gauge.

Gauge: Rnds 1-3 of Hexagon = 2¼" across.
Each Hexagon = 7¼" across.

Skill Level: ✧✧ Average

HEXAGON (make 72)

Rnd 1: With dk. rose, ch 5, sl st in first ch to form ring, ch 1, 12 sc in ring, join with sl st in first sc (12 sc).

Rnd 2: Working this rnd in **back lps** *(see fig. 1, page 156)*, ch 1, 2 sc in each st around, join (24).

Rnd 3: Ch 1, sc in first 4 sts, ch 2, (sc in next 4 sts, ch 2) around, join, fasten off (24 sc, 6 ch-2 sps).

Rnd 4: Working in **front lps** of rnd 1, join lt. rose with sl st in first st, (ch 4, 3 tr, ch 4, sl st) in same st, sl st in next st, *(sl st, ch 4, 3 tr, ch 4, sl st) in next st, sl st in next st; repeat from * around, join with sl st in first sl st, fasten off (6 petals).

Rnd 5: Join dk. rose with sl st in any sl st between petals, ch 5, sc in each of next 3 tr, ch 5, *sl st in next sl st between petals, ch 5, sc in each of next 3 tr, ch 5; repeat from * around, join with sl st in first sl st, fasten off.

Rnd 6: Working in sts of rnd 3, join green with sl st in 3rd sc of any 4-sc group, ch 3, dc in each sc around with (dc, ch 2, dc) in each ch-2 sp, join with sl st in top of ch-3 (36 dc, 6 ch-2 sps).

Rnds 7-8: Ch 3, dc in each st around with (dc, ch 2, dc) in each ch-2 sp, join, ending with 60 dc and 6 ch-2 sps in last rnd. At end of last rnd, fasten off.

Rnd 9: Join off-white with sl st in first st, ch 3, dc in each st around with (dc, ch 2, dc) in each ch-2 sp, join (72 dc, 6 ch-2 sps).

Rnd 10: Ch 3, dc in each st around with (dc, ch 2, dc) in each ch-2 sp, join, fasten off (84 dc, 6 ch-2 sps).

Optional: Secure petals on rnd 4 to each Motif with Glue 'n Wash, if desired, following manufacturer's instructions.

HALF HEXAGON (make 10)

Row 1: With green, ch 3, sl st in first ch to form ring, ch 3, dc in ring, (ch 2, 2 dc in ring) 2 times, **turn** (6 dc, 2 ch-2 sps).

Rows 2-5: Ch 3, dc in same st, dc in each st across with (dc, ch 2, dc) in each ch-2 sp and 2 dc in top of last ch-3, turn, ending with 30 dc

Continued on page 110

ASSEMBLY DIAGRAM

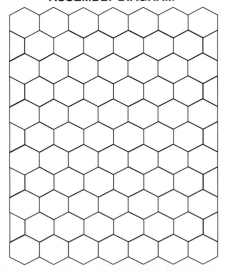

Rosebuds

Finished Size: 46½" x 59"

Materials: Worsted-weight yarn — 39½ oz. white, 5 oz. lilac and 4 oz. rose; I crochet hook or size needed to obtain gauge.

Gauge: 3 sts = 1";
3 sc rows and 2 dc rows = 2".

Skill Level: ✧ Easy

AFGHAN

Row 1: With lilac, ch 142, dc in 4th ch from hook, dc in each ch across, turn (140 dc).

Row 2: Ch 1, sc in each st across, turn.

Row 3: Ch 3, dc in each st across, turn.

Row 4: Ch 1, sc in each st across, turn, fasten off.

Row 5: Join rose with sl st in first st, ch 3, dc in each st across, turn.

Row 6: Repeat row 2, fasten off.

Row 7: With white, repeat row 5.

Row 8: Repeat row 2.

Row 9: Repeat row 3.

Row 10: Repeat row 2, fasten off.

Row 11: Join lilac with sc in first st, sc in next 7 sts, (skip next st, 2 dc in next st, ch 1, 2 dc in next st, skip next st, sc in next 8 sts) across, **do not** turn, fasten off (96 sc, 44 dc, 11 ch-1 sps).

Row 12: Join white with sc in first st, sc in next 7 sts, (ch 4, skip next 4 dc, sc in next 8 sts) across, turn (96 sc, 11 ch-4 sps).

Row 13: Ch 1, sc in each st across with 4 sc in each ch-4 sp, turn, fasten off (140 sc).

Row 14: Join rose with sc in first st, sc in next 7 sts; *working in front of last 2 rows, (2 tr, ch 5, sl st in 5th ch from hook, 2 tr) in next ch-1 sp 3 rows below, skip next 4 sts on last row, sc in next 8 sts; repeat from * across, turn, fasten off (96 sc, 44 tr).

Row 15: Join white with sc in first st, sc in next 7 sts; (working in skipped sts on row before last, dc in next 4 sts; working on last row, sc in next 8 sts) across, turn (140 sts).

Rows 16-21: Repeat rows 3 and 2 alternately. At end of last row, fasten off.

Row 22: Join lilac with sc in first st, sc in next 13 sts, skip next st, 2 dc in next st, ch 1, 2 dc in next st, skip next st, (sc in next 8 sts, skip next st, 2 dc in next st, ch 1, 2 dc in next st, skip next st) 9 times, sc in last 14 sts, **do not** turn, fasten off (100 sc, 40 dc, 10 ch-1 sps).

Row 23: Join white with sc in first st, sc in next 13 sts, ch 4, skip next 4 dc, (sc in next 8 sts, ch 4, skip next 4 dc) 9 times, sc in last 14 sts, turn (100 sc, 10 ch-4 sps).

Row 24: Repeat row 13 (140 sc).

Row 25: Join rose with sc in first st, sc in next 13 sts; *[working in front of last 2 rows, (2 tr, ch 5, sl st in 5th ch from hook, 2 tr) in next ch-1 sp 3 rows below, skip next 4 sts on last row], sc in next 8 sts; repeat from * 8 more times; repeat between [ ], sc in last 14 sts, turn, fasten of (100 sc, 40 tr).

Row 26: Join white with sc in first st, sc in next 13 sts; (*working in skipped sts on row before last, dc in next 4 sts*; working on last row, sc in next 8 sts) 9 times; repeat between **; working on last row, sc in last 14 sts, turn (140 sts).

Rows 27-32: Repeat rows 3 and 2 alternately. At end of last row, fasten off.

Rows 33-48: Repeat rows 11-26.

Continued on page 110

Rosebuds

Continued from page 109

Rows 49-102: Repeat rows 3 and 2 alternately. At end of last row, fasten off.

Rows 103-140: Repeat rows 11-48.

Rows 141-146: Repeat rows 3 and 2 alternately. At end of last row, fasten off.

Rows 147-148: Repeat rows 5 and 6.

Row 149: With lilac, repeat row 5.

Rows 150-152: Repeat rows 2-4.❧

Floating Gardens

Continued from page 103

top of ch-3, ending with 128 dc in last rnd. At end of last rnd, fasten off.

To **assemble,** holding Motifs right sides up, matching sts and working through both thicknesses in **back lps** only, using lt. teal, **reverse sc** *(see fig. 15, page 158)* Motifs together in five rows of six Motifs each.

BORDER

Rnd 1: Working around outer edge in **back lps** only, with right side of afghan facing you, join lt. plum with sc in any center corner st, 2 sc in same st, sc in each st and in each seam around with 3 sc in each center corner st, join with sl st in first sc, fasten off.

Rnd 2: Working in **both lps,** join dk. plum with sc in first sc, sc in each st around with 3 sc in 2nd st of each 3-sc corner, join with sl st in first sc.

Rnd 3: Ch 1, sc in each st around with 3 sc in 2nd st of each 3-sc corner, join, **turn,** fasten off.

Rnd 4: Join dk. teal with sl st in 2nd st of any 3-sc corner, ch 3, 2 dc in same st, skip next 2 sts, *(sl st, ch 3, 2 dc) in next st, skip next 2 sts; repeat from * around to last one or 2 sts, skip last one or 2 sts, join with sl st in first sl st, fasten off.❧

Floral Chambers

Continued from page 107

and 2 ch-2 sps in last row. At end of last row, fasten off.

Rnd 6: Join off-white with sl st in first st, ch 3, dc in same st, dc in each st across with (dc, ch 2, dc) in each ch-2 sp and 2 dc in top of last ch-3, turn (36 dc, 2 ch-2 sps).

Rnd 7: Ch 3, dc in same st, dc in each st across with (dc, ch 2, dc) in each ch-2 sp and 2 dc in top of last ch-3, fasten off (42 dc, 2 ch-2 sps).

To **assemble,** matching sts and ch-2 sps, working in **back lps** only, sew Hexagons and Half Hexagons together as shown in Assembly Diagram on page 107.

EDGING

Rnd 1: Working around entire outer edge of afghan, join off-white with sc in first dc after either short side (see diagram), *sc in each st, in each ch-2 sp and 2 sc in end of each row and ring on Half Hexagons across long edge to next corner, 3 sc in corner ch-2 sp, sc in next 14 dc, 3 sc in next ch-2 sp, (sc in next 14 dc, skip next 2 ch-2 sps, sc in next 14 dc, 3 sc in next ch-2 sp) 6 times, sc in next 14 dc, 3 sc in next corner ch-2 sp; repeat from *, join with sl st in first sc.

Notes: For **triple picot shell (tr-p shell),** sl st in next st, (ch 3, tr, ch 3, sl st) 3 times in same st.

Rnd 2: Ch 1, sc in each st around with tr-p shell in 2nd sc of each 3-sc group across short ends, join, fasten off.❧

Lily of the Nile
Continued from page 104

For **2-dc shell,** (2 dc, ch 2, 2 dc) in next ch sp or st.

For **3-dc shell,** (3 dc, ch 3, 3 dc) in next ch sp or st.

Rnd 2 (Part A): Working across top edge of afghan, sl st in first ch-2 sp, ch 1, (sc, ch 2, sc) in same sp, [(ch 1, sc in next ch sp) 2 times, skip next ch sp, 2-dc shell in next sc, skip next ch sp, (sc in next ch sp, ch 1) 2 times, (sc, ch 2, sc) in next ch-2 sp, (ch 1, sc in next ch sp) 2 times, *skip next ch sp, 2-dc shell in next sc, skip next ch sp, sc in next ch sp*, skip next ch sp, 2-dc shell in next ch sp above seam, skip next ch sp, sc in next ch sp, skip next ch sp, 3-dc shell in next sc, skip next ch sp, sc in next ch sp, skip next ch sp, 2-dc shell in next ch sp above seam, skip next ch sp, sc in next ch sp; repeat between **, ch 1, sc in next ch sp, ch 1, (sc, ch 2, sc) in next ch-2 sp]; repeat between [ ] 3 more times, (ch 1, sc in next ch sp) 2 times, skip next ch sp, 2-dc shell in next sc, skip next ch sp, (sc in next ch sp, ch 1) 2 times;

Rnd 2 (Part B): Working across first long edge, (sc, ch 2, sc) in next ch-2 sp, (ch 1, sc in next ch sp) 2 times, *[skip next ch sp, 2-dc shell in next sc, skip next ch sp, (sc in next ch sp, ch 1) 2 times, (sc, ch 2, sc) in next ch-2 sp, (ch 1, sc in next ch sp) 2 times, skip next ch sp, 2-dc shell in next sc, skip next ch sp, sc in next ch sp], skip next ch sp, 2-dc shell in ch sp above seam, skip

next ch sp, sc in next ch sp; repeat from * 9 more times; repeat between [ ], ch 1, sc in next ch sp, ch 1;

Rnd 2 (Part C): Working across bottom edge, (sc, ch 2, sc) in next ch-2 sp; work between [ ] in Part A 4 times, (ch 1, sc in next ch sp) 2 times, skip next ch sp, 2-dc shell in next sc, skip next ch sp, (sc in next ch sp, ch 1) 2 times;

Rnd 2 (Part D): Working across last long edge, repeat Part B, join with sl st in first sc, fasten off.

Note: For **sc shell,** (sc, ch 2, sc) in next ch sp.

Rnd 3: Join dk. green with sc in first ch-2 sp, ch 2, sc in same sp, ◊[ch 4, skip next 2 sc, sc in next sc, *ch 2, sc shell in next ch-2 sp, ch 2, sc in next sc*, ch 4, skip next 2 sc, sc shell in next ch-2 sp, ch 4, skip next 2 sc, sc in next sc; repeat between ** 2 times, ch 4, sc shell in next ch-3 sp, ch 4, sc in next sc; repeat between ** 2 more times, ch 4, skip next 2 sc, sc shell in next ch-2 sp]; repeat between [ ] 3 more times, (ch 4, skip next 2 sc, sc in next sc, ch 2, sc shell in next ch-2 sp, ch 2, sc in next sc, ch 4, skip next 2 sc, sc shell in next ch sp) 2 times, (ch 4, skip next 2 sc, sc in next sc; repeat between ** 3 more times, ch 4, skip next 2 sc, sc shell in next ch-2 sp) 10 times, ch 4, skip next 2 sc, sc in next sc, ch 2, sc shell in next ch-2 sp, ch 2, sc in next sc, ch 4, skip next 2 sc◊, sc shell in next ch-2 sp; repeat between ◊◊, join, fasten off.

Morning Glory
Continued from page 100

ch sp on last Motif) 2 times, sc in next ch sp on this Motif, (ch 5, sc in next ch sp) 3 times; joining to side of last Motif made on this row, work joining ch sp in 18th ch sp on last Motif, (sc in next ch sp on this Motif, work joining ch sp in next ch sp on last Motif) 2 times, join with sl st in first sc, fasten off.

Repeat Second Motif four more times for a total of six Motifs.

Repeat Second Row seven more times for a total of nine Rows.

FILLER MOTIF

With white, ch 6, sl st in first ch to form ring, ch 1, sc in ring; working in 12 unworked ch-5 sps between 4 joined Motifs, ch 4, drop lp from hook, insert hook in any ch-5 sp, pick up dropped lp, ch 5, (sc in ring, ch 4, drop lp from hook, insert hook in next ch-5 sp, pick up dropped lp, ch 5) 11 times, join with sl st in first sc, fasten off.

Repeat Filler Motif between joined Motifs.

Fascinating images of light and dark
collide in a kaleidoscope that catches your
eye and holds your attention. Polished,
yet playful, these artistic visions of crochet
brilliance reflect a time-honored craft with
a modern touch. A clever combination
of mastery and motion, this exhibit of
ingenious compositions will illuminate your
decor with skillfully adapted patterns
harmoniously crafted for maximum effect.

Indulgent
Illusions

Medallions

Finished Size: 45" x 71" without fringe

Materials: Worsted-weight yarn — 25 oz. white, 18 oz. brown and 14 oz. orange; H crochet hook or size needed to obtain gauge.

Gauge: Rnd 1 of Block = 2" across.

Skill Level: ✧✧ Average

BLOCK (make 35, see Note)

Note: Work Blocks in following colors: 11 orange and white [*Black* / *GREY*], 10 white and brown [*GREY*], 8 brown and white [*Black*], 6 white and orange (see Assembly Diagram on page 128).

For **beginning V-stitch (beg V-st),** ch 4, dc in same st or sp.

For **V-stitch (V-st),** (dc, ch 1, dc) in next st or sp.

Rnd 1: With first color, ch 5, sl st in first ch to form ring, ch 4, (dc in ring, ch 1) 12 times, join with sl st in 3rd ch of ch-4 (13 dc, 13 ch-1 sps).

Rnd 2: Sl st in first ch-1 sp, beg V-st, V-st in each ch-1 sp around, join with sl st in 3rd ch of ch-4 (13 V-sts).

Rnd 3: Sl st in ch sp of first V-st, beg V-st, V-st in next space between V-sts, (V-st in ch sp of each of next 2 V-sts, V-st in next space between V-sts) around, join (20 V-sts).

Rnd 4: Sl st in first V-st, beg V-st, V-st in each V-st around, join, fasten off.

Rnd 5: Join 2nd color with sl st in any V-st; for **beginning corner,** ch 4, (dc, ch 1, V-st) in same sp, V-st in next 4 V-sts; *for **corner,** (V-st, ch 1, V-st) in next V-st, V-st in next 4 V-sts; repeat from * around, join (24 V-sts, 4 corner ch-1 sps).

Rnds 6-8: Sl st in first V-st, beg V-st, V-st in each V-st around with (V-st, ch 1, V-st) in each corner ch-1 sp, join, ending with 48 V-sts and 4 corner ch-1 sps in last rnd. At end of last rnd, fasten off.

To **assemble,** matching sts and ch sps, working in **back lps** *(see fig. 1, page 156),* sew Blocks together in five rows of seven Blocks each as shown in diagram.

BORDER

Rnd 1: Working around entire outer edge of afghan, join brown with sc in any corner ch sp, 2 sc in same sp, sc in each dc and in ch sp before and after each seam around with 3 sc in each corner ch sp, join with sl st in first sc, fasten off.

Rnd 2: Join white with sc in 2nd st of any 3-sc corner, sc in each st around with 3 sc in 2nd st of each 3-sc corner, join, fasten off.

For **each fringe,** cut two strands yarn each 16" long. With both strands held together, fold in half, insert hook in st, draw fold through, draw all loose ends through fold, tighten. Trim ends.

Working in color sequence of brown, orange and white, fringe in every other st across short ends of afghan.❧

Diagram on page 128

Lilac Moments

Finished Size: 47" x 63"

Materials: Worsted-weight yarn — 20½ oz. dk. lavender, 18 oz. lt. lavender and 17 oz. mint; tapestry needle; H crochet hook or size needed to obtain gauge.

Gauge: 7 sts = 2"; 2 dc rnds = 1". Each Square is 8" square.

Skill Level: ✧✧ Average

SQUARE
(make 18 dk. lavender and 17 lt. lavender)

Row 1: With lt. or dk. lavender, ch 26, sc in 2nd ch from hook, sc in each ch across, turn (25 sc).

Row 2: Ch 3, 2 dc in same st, skip next 2 sts, sc in next st, skip next 2 sts, (5 dc in next st, skip next 2 sts, sc in next st, skip next 2 sts) across to last st, 3 dc in last st, turn (21 dc, 4 sc).

Row 3: Ch 1, sc in first st, 5 dc in next sc, (sc in 3rd dc of next 5-dc group, 5 dc in next sc) across to last 3 sts, skip next 2 sts, sc in last st, turn (20 dc, 5 sc).

Row 4: Ch 3, 2 dc in same st, (sc in 3rd dc of next 5-dc group, 5 dc in next sc) 3 times, sc in 3rd dc of next 5-dc group, 3 dc in last st, turn.

Row 5: Ch 1, sc in each of first 2 sts, (*hdc in next st, dc in next st, hdc in next st*, sc in each of next 3 sts) 3 times; repeat between **, sc in each of last 2 sts, turn (25 sts).

Row 6: Ch 3, dc in each of next 2 sts, hdc in each of next 3 sts, sc in next 13 sts, hdc in each of next 3 sts, dc in each of last 3 sts, turn.

Row 7: Ch 3, dc in each of first 2 sts, hdc in each of next 3 sts, sc in each of next 3 sts, sl st in next 7 sts, sc in each of next 3 sts, hdc in each of next 3 sts, dc in each of last 3 sts, **do not** turn, fasten off.

Row 8: Join mint with sc in first st, sc in each of next 2 sts, hdc in each of next 3 sts, dc in each of next 3 sts, tr in next 7 sts, dc in each of next 3 sts, hdc in each of next 3 sts, sc in each of last 3 sts, **do not** turn, fasten off.

Row 9: Working in starting chs on opposite side of row 1, using same color as row 1, join with sc in first ch, sc in each ch across, turn (25 sc).

Rows 10-16: Repeat rows 2-8.

Rnd 17: Working around outer edge, join green with sc in first st on last row, (sc in each st across, ch 3; working in ends of rows, evenly space 25 sc across, ch 3) 2 times, join with sl st in first sc, fasten off (25 sc on each edge between corner ch sps).

For **first, third and fifth strips,** holding Squares vertically starting with dk. lavender and alternating colors, with mint, sew four dk. lavender and three lt. lavender Squares together through **back lps.**

For **second and fourth strips,** holding Squares horizontally, starting with lt. lavender and alternationg colors, with mint, sew four lt. lavender and three dk. lavender Squares together through **back lps** (*see fig. 1, page 156*).

With mint, sew strips together through **back lps.**

BORDER

Rnd 1: Working around entire outer edge, join mint with sc in 12th st past any corner ch sp on one long edge, ch 1, skip next st, (sc in next st, ch 1, skip next st) 6 times, [◊*sc in

Continued on page 129

BY SHARI L. JACOBSON

Peacock Splendor

Finished Size: 48" x 64"
without tassels

Materials: Worsted-weight yarn — 14 oz. blue,
12 oz. green, 10½ oz. tan, 9 oz. each navy and lavender;
metallic blending filament — 8 spools bright blue; 6" piece
of cardboard; H crochet hook or size needed to obtain gauge.

Gauge: 10 dc sts = 3"; 4 dc rows = 2"

Skill Level: ✧✧ Average

STRIP (make 5)

Note: When pattern calls for navy/filament, use one strand each navy worsted and blending filament held together.

Rnd 1: With navy/filament, ch 3, sl st in first ch to form ring, ch 1, 7 sc in ring, join with sl st in first sc (7 sc).

Rnd 2: Ch 1, 2 sc in each st around, join (14).

Note: For **long sc,** working over sts on last 2 rnds, insert hook, yo, draw up long lp, yo, draw through both lps on hook.

Rnd 3: Ch 1, 2 sc in first st, sc in next st, (2 sc in next st, sc in next st) 5 times changing to blue in last st made (*see fig. 9, page 158*), 3 long sc in center of beginning ring on rnd 1 changing to navy/filament in last st made, skip last 2 sts on last rnd, join with sl st in first sc (18 sc, 3 long sc).

Rnd 4: Ch 1, 2 sc in first st, sc in each of next 3 sts, (2 sc in next st, sc in each of next 3 sts) 3 times, 2 sc in next st, sc in next st changing to blue in last st made, sc in next st, 2 sc in next st, sc in last st, join, fasten off navy/filament (27 sc).

Rnd 5: Ch 1, sc in each of first 2 sts, 2 sc in next st, (sc in next 4 sts, 2 sc in next st) 3 times, sc in next 5 sts, 2 sc in next st, sc in each of last 3 sts, join, fasten off (32).

Rnd 6: Join green with sc in first st, 2 sc in next st, (sc in next 5 sts, 2 sc in next st) 4 times, sc in last 6 sts, join, fasten off (37).

Rnd 7: Join tan with sc in first st, (sc in each of next 2 sts, 2 sc in next st) 2 times, hdc in each of next 2 sts, 2 hdc in next st, (dc in each of next 2 sts, 2 dc in next st) 2 times, dc in each of next 3 sts, (2 dc in next st, dc in each of next 2 sts) 2 times, 2 hdc in next st, hdc in each of next 2 sts, 2 sc in next st, sc in each of next 2 sts, 2 sc in next st, sc in next 4 sts, 2 sc in last st, join (48 sts).

Rnd 8: Ch 1, 2 sc in first st, sc in next 4 sts, 2 sc in next st, sc in next 5 sts, hdc in next 4 sts, 2 dc in next st, (dc in each of next 3 sts, 2 dc in next st) 3 times, hdc in next 4 sts, (sc in next 5 sts, 2 sc in next st) 2 times, sc in last 4 sts, join (56).

Rnd 9: Ch 1, sc in first 16 sts, hdc in each of next 2 sts, 2 hdc in next st, hdc in each of next 2 sts, 2 dc in next st, dc in next st, 2 dc in next st, dc in each of next 3 sts, 2 dc in next st, dc in next st, 2 dc in next st, hdc in each of next 2 sts, 2 hdc in next st, hdc in each of next 2 sts, sc in next 16 sts, hdc in each of next 2 sts, 3 dc in next st, hdc in each of last 2 sts, join, fasten off (64).

Rnd 10: Join navy/filament with sc in first st, sc in next 21 sts, 2 hdc in next st, hdc in next 4 sts, dc in next st, (dc, ch 1, dc) in next st, dc in next st, hdc in next 4 sts, 2 hdc in next st, sc in next 22 sts, hdc in each of next 2 sts, dc in next st, (dc, ch 2, dc) in next st, dc in next st, hdc in each of last 2 sts, join, fasten off

Continued on page 130

Shimmering Dewdrops

Finished Size: 51" x 69"
without fringe

Materials: Worsted-weight yarn — 32 oz. lt. blue;
3-ply sport pompadour yarn — 43 oz. white;
I crochet hook or size needed to obtain gauge.

Gauge: With worsted-weight, 3 dc sts = 1".
One dc row and one sc row = 1" tall.

Skill Level: ✧✧ Average

AFGHAN

Row 1: With lt. blue, ch 155, dc in 4th ch from hook, dc in each ch across, turn (153 dc).

Row 2: Ch 1, sc in each st across, turn, fasten off.

Note: Work white rows using 2 strands sport yarn held together.

For **treble crochet front post (tr fp)** (*see fig. 14, page 158*), yo 2 times, insert hook from front to back around post of next st, yo, draw lp through, complete as tr, skip next st on row you are working behind fp.

For **double treble crochet front post (dtr fp),** yo 3 times, insert hook from front to back around post of next st, yo, draw lp through, (yo, draw through 2 lps on hook) 4 times, skip next st on row you are working behind fp.

Row 3: Join white with sl st in first st, ch 3, dc in each of next 2 sts, *tr fp around next st on row before last, dtr fp around next st on row before last, tr fp around next st on row before last, dc in each of next 3 sts on last row; repeat from * across, **do not** turn, fasten off (78 dc, 50 tr fp, 25 dtr fp).

Row 4: Join lt. blue with sl st in first st, ch 3, dc in each st across, turn (153 dc).

Row 5: Ch 1, sc in each st across, turn, fasten off.

Row 6: Join white with sl st in first st, ch 3, dc in next 5 sts, *(tr fp around next st on row before last, dtr fp around next st on row before last, tr fp around next st on row before last), dc in each of next 3 sts; repeat from * across to last 9 sts; repeat between ( ), dc in last 6 sts, **do not** turn, fasten off (81 dc, 48 tr fp, 24 dtr fp).

Rows 7-8: Repeat rows 4 and 5.

Rows 9-137: Repeat rows 3-8 consecutively, ending with row 5.

For **each fringe,** cut three strands white each 7" long. With all 3 strands held together, fold in half, insert hook in st, draw fold through, draw all loose ends through fold, tighten. Trim ends.

Fringe in every stitch on short ends of afghan.🖙

Jeweltone Treasures

Finished Size: 47" x 60½"

Materials: Worsted-weight yarn — 32½ oz. red,
20½ oz. blue and 13 oz. green; tapestry needle;
G crochet hook or size needed to obtain gauge.

Gauge: 4 sc = 1"; rnds 1-5 of Small Square = 2¼".
Each Small Block is 5¾" square.

Skill Level: ✧✧ Average

LARGE SQUARE (make 12)
Small Square (make 4)

Rnd 1: With red, ch 4, sl st in first ch to form ring, ch 1, 8 sc in ring, join with sl st in first sc (8 sc).

Rnd 2: Ch 1, (sc, ch 5, sc) in first st, ch 5, skip next st, *(sc, ch 5, sc) in next st, ch 5, skip next st; repeat from * around, join, fasten off (8 sc, 8 ch sps).

Rnd 3: Working in skipped sts on rnd 1, behind sts on last rnd, join blue with sc in first skipped st, ch 3, (sc in next skipped st, ch 3) 3 times, join with sl st in first sc (4 sc, 4 ch sps).

Notes: For **beginning shell (beg shell),** ch 3, (dc, ch 2, 2 dc) in same st.

For **shell,** (2 dc, ch 2, 2 dc) in next st.

Rnd 4: Beg shell, sc in next ch sp; *shell in next st; sc in next ch sp; repeat from * around, join with sl st in top of ch-3 (4 shells, 4 sc).

Rnd 5: Ch 1, sc in each st around with (sc, ch 2, sc) in each corner ch sp, join with sl st in first sc, fasten off (28 sc, 4 ch sps).

Rnd 6: Join red with sc in first st, sc in each of next 2 sts, *[(sc, ch 2, sc) in next ch sp, sc in each of next 3 sts, sc in next st and in next skipped ch-5 sp on rnd 2 at same time], sc in each of next 3 sts; repeat from * 2 times; repeat between [ ], join (36 sc, 4 ch sps).

Rnd 7: Repeat rnd 5, **turn,** fasten off (44 sc, 4 ch sps).

Rnd 8: Join green with sc in any corner ch-2 sp, ch 2, sc in same sp, sc in each st around with (sc, ch 2, sc) in each corner ch sp, join, **turn** (52 sc, 4 ch sps).

Rnd 9: Sl st in next st, ch 1, sc in same st, ch 1, skip next st, (sc in next st, ch 1, skip next st) 6 times, *[(sc, ch 2, sc) in next ch sp, ch 1, skip next st, (sc in next st, ch 1, skip next st) across] to next corner ch sp; repeat from *; repeat between [ ], join, fasten off (32 sc, 28 ch-1 sps, 4 ch-2 sps).

Rnd 10: Join blue with sc in first ch sp, sc in each st and in each ch-1 sp around with (sc, ch 2, sc) in each corner ch-2 sp, join, **turn** (68 sc, 4 ch sps).

Rnd 11: Repeat rnd 5, **turn** (76 sc, 4 ch sps).

Note: For **treble front post stitch (fp)** *(see fig. 14, page 158),* yo 2 times, insert hook from right to left around post of next st 3 rnds below, yo, draw lp through, (yo, draw through 2 lps on hook) 3 times.

Rnd 12: Join red with sc in any ch sp, ch 3, sc in same sp, *[sc in each of next 2 sts, fp, sc in each of next 3 sts, fp, sc in next 5 sts, fp, sc in each of next 3 sts, fp, sc in each of next 2 sts], (sc, ch 3, sc) in next ch sp; repeat from * 2 more times; repeat between [ ], join, fasten off (84 sts, 4 ch sps).

With red, sew four Small Squares together through **back lps** *(see fig. 1, page 156)* only forming one Large Square.

Edging

Rnd 1: Working around outer edge of Large

Continued on page 131

Ebb & Flow

Finished Size: 45" x 72"
without Tassels

Materials: Worsted-weight yarn — 28 oz. black
and 25 oz. white; tapestry needle;
K crochet hook or size needed to obtain gauge.

Gauge: 2 pattern sts (see Note) = 1";
3 pattern st rows = 1¼"

Skill Level: ✧ Easy

AFGHAN

Note: For **pattern stitch (patt st),** (sc, hdc) in next ch, hdc or sc.

Row 1: With black, ch 191, 2 hdc in 2nd ch from hook, *[skip next ch, (patt st in next ch, skip next ch) 5 times, hdc in next ch, skip next 2 chs, hdc in next ch, skip next ch, (patt st in next ch, skip next ch) 5 times], 3 hdc in next ch; repeat from * 5 more times; repeat between [ ], 2 hdc in last st, turn (70 patt sts, 36 hdc).

Rows 2-3: Ch 1, 2 hdc in first st, *[(patt st, skip next st) 5 times, hdc in next st, skip next 2 sts, hdc in next st, (patt st, skip next st) 5 times], 3 hdc in next st; repeat from * 5 more times; repeat between [ ], 2 hdc in last st, turn. At end of last row, fasten off.

Row 4: Join white with sl st in first st, ch 1, 2 hdc in first st, *[(patt st, skip next st) 5 times, hdc in next st, skip next 2 sts, hdc in next st, (patt st, skip next st) 5 times], 3 hdc in next st; repeat from * 5 more times; repeat between [ ], 2 hdc in last st, turn.

Rows 5-6: Repeat rows 2-3.

Row 7: Join black with sl st in first st, ch 1, 2 hdc in first st, *[(patt st, skip next st) 5 times, hdc in next st, skip next 2 sts, hdc in next st, (patt st, skip next st) 5 times], 3 hdc in next st; repeat from * 5 more times; repeat between [ ], 2 hdc in last st, turn.

Rows 8-9: Repeat rows 2-3.

Rows 10-135: Repeat rows 4-9 consecutively.

TASSEL
(make 7 each black and white)

For **each Tassel,** cut 22 strands yarn each 7" long. Tie separate strand tightly around middle of all strands. Wrap 10" strand 1¼" from top of fold, secure. Trim ends.

Tie Tassel to each point across short ends of afghan, alternating colors.❧

Desert Reflections

Finished Size: 46" x 63½"
not including Fringe

Materials: Worsted-weight yarn — 30 oz. off-white, 12 oz. each
blue/rose print, solid rose, solid blue and blue/rose ombre;
tapestry needle; F crochet hook or size needed to obtain gauge.

Gauge: 9 sc sts = 2"; 4 sc back lp rows = 1".

Skill Level: ✧✧ Average

PANEL A (make 4)
Strip (make 2)

Notes: At the end of each row, **do not** turn, fasten off leaving 6" end for fringe.

All sc sts are worked in **back lps** (*see fig. 1, page 156*) unless otherwise stated.

For **variation double crochet (vdc),** dc in **front lp** of next st on third row below.

Row 1: With off-white, ch 285, fasten off. Join off-white with sc in first ch, sc in each ch across (285 sc).

Rows 2-5: Join off-white with sc in first st, sc in each st across.

Row 6: Join solid rose with sc in first st, sc in next 6 sts, vdc, (sc in next 9 sts, vdc) 27 times, sc in last 7 sts (257 sc, 28 vdc).

Row 7: Join print with sc in first st, sc in next 5 sts, vdc, sc in next st, vdc, (sc in next 7 sts, vdc, sc in next st, vdc) 27 times, sc in last 6 sts (229 sc, 56 vdc).

Row 8: Join solid blue with sc in first st, sc in next 4 sts, vdc, sc in each of next 3 sts, vdc, (sc in next 5 sts, vdc, sc in each of next 3 sts, vdc) 27 times, sc in last 5 sts.

Rows 9-10: Join off-white with sc in first st, sc in each st across.

Row 11: With solid blue, repeat row 6.

Row 12: Repeat row 7.

Row 13: With rose, repeat row 8.

Holding Strips wrong sides together, matching row 13, working through both thicknesses, with rose, sew **back lps** of sts together.

PANEL B (make 3)
Strip (make 2)

Rows 1-5: Repeat same rows of Strip on Panel A.

Row 6: With solid blue, repeat same row of Strip on Panel A.

Row 7: Repeat same row of Strip on Panel A.

Row 8: With solid rose, repeat same row of Strip on Panel A.

Rows 9-10: Repeat same rows of Strip on Panel A.

Rows 11-13: Repeat rows 6-8 of Strip on Panel A.

Holding Strips wrong sides together, matching row 13, working through both thicknesses, with blue, sew **back lps** of sts together.

ASSEMBLY

To **join Panel A to Panel B,** working in starting chs on opposite side of row 1 on both pieces, with wrong sides facing you, join ombre with sc in first ch on Panel A, ch 1, sc in first ch on Panel B, (ch 1, sc in next ch on Panel A, ch 1, sc in next ch on Panel B) across, fasten off.

Alternating Panels, join remaining Panels in same manner.

For **edging,** working in starting chs on opposite side of row 1 on one outside Panel, join blue ombre with sl st in first ch, ch 3, dc in each ch across, fasten off.

Repeat on opposite Panel.

Continued on page 129

Medallions

Continued from page 114

ASSEMBLY DIAGRAM

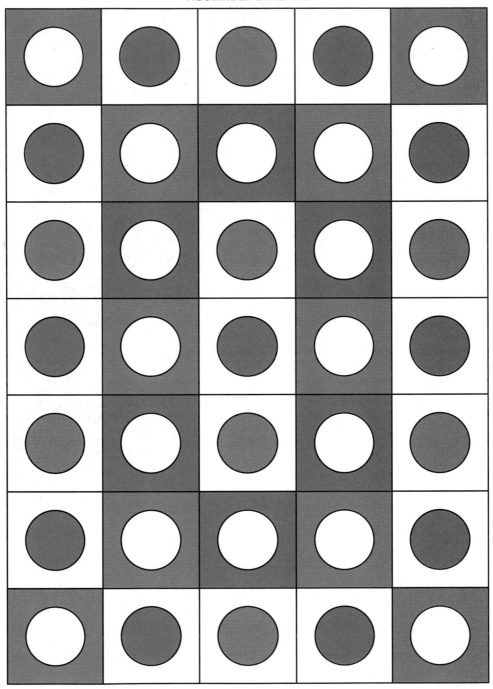

Lilac Moments

Continued from page 117

next ch sp, ch 1, skip next seam, ch 1, sc next ch sp, ch 1, skip next st, (sc in next st, ch 1, skip next st) 12 times; repeat from * across to next corner ch-3 sp, (sc, ch 3, sc) in next ch sp, ch 1, skip next st◊, (sc in next st, ch 1, skip next st) 12 times]; repeat between [ ] 2 times; repeat between ◊◊, (sc in next st, ch 1, skip next st) 5 times, join with sl st in first sc (98 sc and 97 ch-1 sps on each long edge between corner ch-3 sps, 70 sc and 69 ch-1 sps on each short edge between each corner ch-3 sp).

Rnd 2: Ch 1, sc in each st and in each ch-1 sp around with (sc, ch 3, sc) in each corner ch-3 sp, join (197 sc on each long edge between corner ch-3 sps, 141 sc on each short edge between each corner ch-3 sp).

Rnd 3: Join lt. lavender with sc in 15th st on long edge past corner ch sp, skip next 2 sts, *(5 dc in next st, skip next 2 sts, sc in next st, skip next 2 sts) across to next corner ch sp, 7 dc in next ch sp, skip next st, sc in next st, (skip next 2 sts, 5 dc in next st, skip next 2 sts, sc in next st) across to one st before next corner ch sp, skip next st, 7 dc in next ch sp, skip next 2 sts*, sc in next st, skip next 2 sts; repeat between **, (sc in next st, skip next 2 sts, 5 dc in next st, skip next 2 sts) 2 times, join, **turn.**

Rnd 4: Sl st in each of next 3 sts, ch 1, sc in same st, 5 dc in next sc, sc in 3rd dc of next 5-dc group, 5 dc in next sc, *[skip next st, sc in next st, skip next st, 7 dc in next st, skip next st, sc in next st, skip next st, 5 dc in next sc,

(sc in 3rd dc of next 5-dc group, 5 dc in next sc) across] to next corner 7-dc group; repeat from * 2 more times; repeat between [ ], join, **turn,** fasten off.

Rnd 5: Join mint with sc in center dc of 2nd 5-dc group before corner 7-dc group on one long edge, 5 dc in next sc, sc in 3rd dc of next 5-dc group, 5 dc in next sc, *[skip next st, sc in next st, skip next st, 7 dc in next st, skip next st, sc in next st, skip next st, 5 dc in next sc, (sc in 3rd dc of next 5-dc group, 5 dc in next sc) across] to next corner 7-dc group; repeat from * 2 more times; repeat between [ ], join, **do not** turn, fasten off.

Rnd 6: With lavender, repeat rnd 5, **turn, do not** fasten off.

Rnd 7: Sl st in each of next 3 sts, ch 1, sc in same st, *[5 dc in next sc, (sc in 3rd dc of next 5-dc group, 5 dc in next sc) across] to next corner 7-dc group, skip next st, sc in next st, skip next st, 7 dc in next st, skip next st, sc in next st, skip next st; repeat from * 3 more times; repeat between [ ], join, **turn.**

Rnd 8: Ch 1, sc in first st, [*ch 3, (sc, ch 3, sc) in 3rd dc of next 5-dc group, ch 3, sc in next sc; repeat from * across to next corner 7-dc group, ch 2, skip next 2 sts, sc in next st, ch 3, (sc, ch 3, sc) in next st, ch 3, sc in next st, ch 2, skip next 2 sts, sc in next sc]; repeat between [ ] 3 times, ch 3, (sc, ch 3, sc) in 3rd dc of next 5-dc group, ch 3, ◊sc in next sc, ch 3, (sc, ch 3, sc) in 3rd dc of next 5-dc group, ch 3◊; repeat between ◊◊ across, join, fasten off.☙

Desert Reflections

Continued from page 127

FRINGE

For **each Fringe,** cut one strand solid rose, solid blue and off-white each 13" long. With all strands held together, fold in half, insert hook in end of row at center of a group of

three 6" ends, draw fold through row, draw all loose ends including 6" ends through fold, tighten. Trim ends.

Fringe in end of each row at center of a group of three 6" ends on each short end of Afghan.☙

Peacock Splendor

Continued from page 118

(68 sts, 1 ch-2 sp, 1 ch-1 sp).

Note: Ch-3 counts as first dc of each row or rnd.

Rnd 11: Join blue with sl st in ch-2 sp, ch 3, dc in same sp, *dc in next 12 sts, 2 dc in next st, dc in next 8 sts, 2 dc in next st, dc in next 12 sts*, (dc, tr, ch 2, tr, dc) in next ch-1 sp; repeat between **, 2 dc in same ch-2 sp as first st, ch 2, join with sl st in top of ch-3 (80 sts, 2 ch-2 sps).

Row 12: Skip first 30 sts, mark next st, **turn;** working in rows, join green with sl st in marked st, ch 4, dc in same st, dc in next 12 sts, 2 dc in next st, dc in next 17 sts, (2 dc, ch 2, 2 dc) in next ch-2 sp, dc in next 17 sts, 2 dc in next st, dc in next 12 sts, (dc, ch 1, dc) in next st leaving remaining sts unworked, **turn,** fasten off (70 dc, 2 ch-1 sps, 1 ch-2 sp).

Row 13: Join lavender with sl st in 10th st on last row, ch 4, dc in same st, dc in next 8 sts, 2 dc in next st, dc in next 16 sts, (2 dc, ch 2, 2 dc) in next ch-2 sp, dc in next 16 sts, 2 dc in next st, dc in next 8 sts, (dc, ch 1, dc) in next st leaving remaining sts unworked, turn, fasten off (60 dc, 2 ch-1 sps, 1 ch-2 sp).

Row 14: Join navy/filament with sl st in 13th st on last row, ch 3, dc in next 17 sts, (2 dc, ch 2, 2 dc) in next ch-2 sp, dc in next 18 sts leaving remaining sts unworked, turn, fasten off (40 dc, 1 ch-2 sp).

Note: Work remainder of Strip in the following color sequence: blue, tan, green, lavender, navy/filament, blue, green, tan, lavender, green, blue, lavender, navy/filament and green.

Rows 15-84: Join next color with sl st in 3rd st on last row, ch 3, dc in next 17 sts, (2 dc, ch 2, 2 dc) in next ch-2 sp, dc in next 18 sts, skip last 2 sts, turn, fasten off.

For **spine,** working over center of Strip, with right side facing you, join navy with sl st in center of ch-2 sp on rnd 10, (ch 2 loosely, sl st in center of ch-2 sp on next rnd or row) across, fasten off.

EDGING

Row 1: For **first side,** with right side of Strip facing you, join blue with sc in top of last st on row 14, (ch 2, sc in top of first ch-3 on next row, ch 1, sc in top of last st on next row) across, turn (71 sc, 35 ch-2 sps, 35 ch-1 sps).

Row 2: Ch 1, sc in each st and in each ch across, turn (176 sc).

Row 3: Ch 1, sc in each st across, turn, fasten off.

For **2nd side,** beginning in top of last st on row 84 and working across to row 1, work same as first side.

Repeat Edging on each Strip.

ASSEMBLY

Hold two Strips wrong sides together with "eyes" (rnds 1-10) on opposite ends; matching sts of Edgings, join blue with sl st in end of Edging on front Strip; for tassel loop, ch 6; working through both thicknesses of edgings in **back lps** (see fig. 1, page 156) only, sl st in each st across to opposite end, ch 6, sl st in end of next row on edging, fasten off.

Continuing to alternate direction of Strips as shown in photo, repeat with remaining Strips.

TASSLES
(make 12 blue, 10 lavender, 10 green, 5 navy/filament and 5 blue/filament)

For **each Tassel,** wrap yarn around cardboard 15 times, tie separate strand of yarn through lps on one end (top), cut loops on opposite end. Wrap separate piece of yarn around all strands 1½" from top; trim ends.

Attach one navy/filament Tassel in ch-2 sp on row 84 at end of spine on each Strip. Attach one blue/filament Tassel in ch-2 sp on rnd 11 on opposite end of each Strip. Matching colors, attach remaining Tassels to ends of rows and Tassel loops at each end of seams.

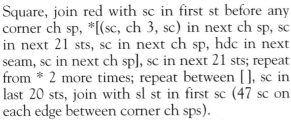

Jeweltone Treasures

Continued from page 123

Square, join red with sc in first st before any corner ch sp, *[(sc, ch 3, sc) in next ch sp, sc in next 21 sts, sc in next ch sp, hdc in next seam, sc in next ch sp], sc in next 21 sts; repeat from * 2 more times; repeat between [ ], sc in last 20 sts, join with sl st in first sc (47 sc on each edge between corner ch sps).

Rnd 2: Ch 1, sc in first st, ch 1, skip next st, *[(sc, ch 3, sc) in next ch sp, ch 1, skip next st, (sc in next st, ch 1, skip next st) across] to next corner ch sp; repeat from * 2 more times; repeat between [ ], join, fasten off (25 sc and 24 ch-1 sps on each edge between corner ch-3 sps).

Rnd 3: Join green with sc in first st, sc in each ch-1 sp and in each st around with (sc, ch 3, sc) in each corner ch-3 sp, join, fasten off (51 sc on each short edge between corner ch sps).

With green, sew Large Squares together through **back lps** only in three rows of four Large Squares each.

BORDER

Rnd 1: Working around entire outer edge, join green with sc in first st before any corner ch sp, sc in each st and in each ch sp before and after seams around with hdc in each seam and (sc, ch 3, sc) in each corner ch sp, join with sl st in first sc (215 sc on each long edge between corner ch sps, 161 sc on each short edge between corner ch sps).

Rnd 2: Repeat same rnd of Edging (109 sc and 108 ch-1 sps on each long edge between corner ch-3 sps, 82 sc and 81 ch-1 sps on each short edge between corner ch-3 sps).

Rnd 3: With blue, repeat same rnd of Edging, **turn, do not** fasten off (219 sc on each long edge between corner ch sps, 165 on each short edge between corner ch sps).

Rnd 4: Ch 1, sc in first st, *ch 1, skip next st, (sc in next st, ch 1, skip next st) across to next corner ch sp, (sc, ch 3, sc) in next ch sp; repeat from * 3 more times, ch 1, skip next st, sc in next st, ch 1, skip last st, join, **turn** (111 sc and 110 ch-1 sps on each long edge between

corner ch-3 sps, 84 sc and 83 ch-1 sps on each short edge between corner ch-3 sps).

Rnd 5: Ch 3, dc in each ch-1 sp and in each st around with shell in each corner ch-3 sp, join with sl st in top of ch-3, **turn** (221 dc on each long edge between corner shells, 167 dc on each short edge between corner shells).

Rnd 6: Sl st in next st, ch 1, sc in same st, *[ch 1, skip next st, (sc in next st, ch 1, skip next st) across] to next corner ch sp, (sc, ch 3, sc) in next ch sp; repeat from * 3 more times; repeat between [ ], join with sl st in first sc, **turn,** fasten off (114 sc and 113 ch-1 sps on each long edge between corner ch-3 sps, 87 sc and 86 ch-1 sps on each short edge between corner ch-3 sps).

Rnd 7: Join red with sc in top right corner ch sp, ch 3, sc in same sp, sc in each st and in each ch-1 sp around with (sc, ch 3, sc) in each corner ch-3 sp, join (229 sc on each long edge between corner ch sps, 175 sc on each short edge between corner ch sps).

Rnd 8: Ch 3, shell in next ch sp, dc in each st around with shell in each corner ch sp, join with sl st in top of ch-3 (229 dc on each long edge between corner shells, 175 dc on each short edge between corner shells).

Rnd 9: Ch 1, sc in first st, skip next 2 sts; *for **corner shell,** (3 dc, ch 3, 3 dc) in next ch sp; skip next 2 sts, sc in next st, skip next 2 sts, (shell in next st, skip next 2 sts, sc in next st, skip next 2 sts) across to next corner ch sp; repeat from * 2 more times; corner shell in next ch sp, skip next 2 sts, (sc in next st, skip next 2 sts, shell in next st, skip next 2 sts) across, join with sl st in first sc.

Rnd 10: Sl st in next 2 sts, ch 1, (sc, ch 3, sc) in same st, [◊ch 3, skip next st, (sc, ch 3, sc) in next ch sp, ch 3, skip next st, (sc, ch 3, sc) in next st, ch 3, skip next st, sc in next sc, ch 3, *(sc, ch 3, sc) in ch sp of next shell, ch 3, sc in next sc, ch 3; repeat from * across◊ to next corner shell, skip next st, (sc, ch 3, sc) in next st]; repeat between [ ] 2 more times; repeat between ◊◊, join, fasten off.

Unveil a treasure trove of sparkling gems
that seem to spring forth from the earth as
do the precious jewels they reflect.
Gleaming with the timeless fire of sap-
phire, topaz, ruby and diamond, these
magnificent accessories of unmistakable
grandeur lend richness to any decor.
Bestow grand eloquence on your domain
with a priceless hand-crafted version of an
ancient symbol of undying devotion.

Diamond Dreams

Sunshine Filet

Finished Size: 45" x 69"

Materials: Worsted-weight yarn — 43 oz. lt. yellow and 18 oz. gold; F crochet hook or size needed to obtain gauge.

Gauge: 17 dc = 4"; 7 dc rows = 3".

Skill Level: ✧✧ Average

AFGHAN

Row 1: With lt. yellow, ch 189, dc in 4th ch from hook, dc in each of next 3 chs, ch 1, skip next ch, (dc in next 7 chs, ch 1, skip next ch) 22 times, dc in last 5 chs, turn (164 dc, 23 ch-1 sps).

Row 2: Ch 3, dc in each of next 3 sts, (*ch 1, skip next st, dc in next ch sp, ch 1, skip next st*, dc in next 5 sts) 22 times; repeat between **, dc in last 4 sts, turn (141 dc, 46 ch-1 sps).

Row 3: Ch 3, dc in each of next 2 sts, (ch 1, skip next st, dc in next ch sp, dc in next st, dc in next ch sp, ch 1, skip next st, dc in each of last 3 sts) across, turn (141 dc, 46 ch-1 sps).

Row 4: Ch 3, dc in next st, (*ch 1, skip next st, dc in next ch sp, dc in each of next 3 sts, dc in next ch sp, ch 1, skip next st, dc in next st) across to last st, dc in last st, turn.

Row 5: Ch 4, skip next st, (dc in next ch sp, dc in next 5 sts, dc in next ch sp, ch 1, skip next st) across to last st, dc in last st, turn (163 dc, 24 ch-1 sps).

Row 6: Ch 3, dc in next ch sp, (ch 1, skip next st, dc in next 5 sts, ch 1, skip next st, dc in next ch sp) across with dc in last st, turn (141, 46 ch-1 sps).

Row 7: Ch 3, dc in next st, dc in next ch sp, (*ch 1, skip next st, dc in each of next 3 sts, ch 1, skip next st, dc in next ch sp, dc in next st*, dc in next ch sp) 22 times; repeat between **, dc in last st, turn.

Row 8: Ch 3, dc in each of next 2 sts, (dc in next ch sp, ch 1, skip next st, dc in next st, ch 1, skip next st, dc in next ch sp, dc in each of next 3 sts) across, turn.

Row 9: Ch 3, dc in each of next 3 sts, (*dc in next ch sp, ch 1, skip next st, dc in next ch sp*, dc in next 5 sts) 22 times; repeat between **, dc in last 4 sts, turn (164 dc, 23 ch-1 sps).

Note: Pattern is established in rows 2-9.

Rows 10-20: Work in pattern ending with row 4. At end of last row, fasten off.

Rows 21-25: Join gold with sl st in first st, work in pattern. At end of last row, fasten off.

Rows 26-44: Join lt. yellow with sl st in first st, work in pattern, ending with row 4. At end of last row, fasten off.

Rows 45-53: Join gold with sl st in first st, work in pattern, ending with row 5. At end of last row, fasten off.

Rows 54-72: Join lt. yellow with sl st in first st, work in pattern, ending with row 8. At end of last row, fasten off.

Rows 73-85: Join gold with sl st in first st, work in pattern, ending with row 5. At end of last row, fasten off.

Rows 86-104: Join lt. yellow with sl st in first st, work in pattern, ending with row 8. At end of last row, fasten off.

Rows 105-113: Join gold with sl st in first st, work in pattern. At end of last row, fasten off.

Rows 114-132: Join lt. yellow with sl st in first st, work in pattern, ending with row 4. At end of last row, fasten off.

Continued on page 146

Cresting Waves

Finished Size: 48" x 59"

Materials: Worsted-weight yarn — 29 oz. each white and navy; G crochet hook or size needed to obtain gauge.

Gauge: 2 shells = 3"; 2 shell rows = 1¾".

Skill Level: ✧ Easy

NAVY STRIP
(make 8)

Notes: For **double treble crochet (dtr),** yo 3 times, insert hook in 5th ch from hook, yo, draw lp through, (yo, draw through 2 lps on hook) 4 times.

For **beginning small shell (beg sm shell),** ch 2, (hdc, dc, ch 2, dc, 2 hdc) in same sp.

For **small shell (sm shell),** (2 hdc, dc, ch 2, dc, 2 hdc) in next ch sp.

For **beginning large shell (beg lg shell),** ch 3, (2 dc, ch 2, 3 dc) in same sp.

For **large shell (lg shell),** (3 dc, ch 2, 3 dc) in next ch sp.

Row 1: For **foundation row,** with navy, ch 5, dtr in 5th ch from hook, (ch 5, dtr in top of last dtr made) 37 times, **do not** turn (38 lps).

Row 2: Working across one side of foundation row, sl st in first lp, beg sm shell, sm shell in next 37 lps, sl st in same lp; working on opposite side of foundation row, sl st in next lp, beg sm shell, sm shell in next 37 lps, **do not** turn, fasten off (38 sm shells on each side of foundation row).

Row 3: Join navy with sl st in ch sp of first shell, beg lg shell, lg shell 37 times leaving remaining shells unworked, fasten off, **do not** turn (38 lg shells).

Row 3: Working across other side of row 2, join navy with sl st in ch sp of first shell, beg lg shell, lg shell 37 times, fasten off (38 lg shells).

CONNECTING STRIP

Row 1: With white, repeat same row of Navy Strip.

Row 2: Working across one side of foundation row, sl st in first lp, ch 2, (hdc, dc) in same lp, ch 2; **to join to Navy Strip,** drop lp from hook, insert hook in ch sp of first shell on Navy Strip, pick up dropped lp, draw lp through sp, ch 1, (dc, 2 hdc) in same lp on this Strip, *(2 hdc, dc) in next lp, ch 2, drop lp from hook, insert hook in ch sp of next shell on Navy Strip, pick up dropped lp, draw lp through sp, ch 1, (dc, 2 hdc) in same lp on this Strip; repeat from *36 more times leaving lps on opposite side unworked, **do not** turn, fasten off (38 joined sm shells).

Row 2: Working across opposite side of foundation row, join white with sl st in first lp, ch 2, (hdc, dc) in same lp, ch 2; **to join to next Navy Strip,** drop lp from hook, insert hook in ch sp of first shell on Navy Strip, pick up dropped lp, draw lp through sp, ch 1, (dc, 2 hdc) in same lp on this Strip, *(2 hdc, dc) in next lp, ch 2, drop lp from hook, insert hook in ch sp of next shell on Navy Strip, pick up dropped lp, draw lp through sp, ch 1, (dc, 2 hdc) in same lp on this Strip; repeat from *36 more times, fasten off (38 joined sm shells).

Repeat Connecting Strip six more times for a total of eight Navy Strips joined by seven Connecting Strips.

Continued on page 146

Rose Delight

Finished Size: 56" x 65"

Materials: Worsted-weight yarn — 36 oz. white, 24 oz. red and 19 oz. black; tapestry needle; I crochet hook or size needed to obtain gauge.

Gauge: 13 sc = 4"; rnd 1 of Triangle = 2¼" across. Each side of Triangle = 9" across.

Skill Level: ✧✧ Average

TRIANGLE (make 66)

Rnd 1: With red, ch 9, sl st in first ch to form ring, ch 3, 2 dc in ring, ch 1, (3 dc in ring, ch 1) 5 times, join with sl st in top of ch-3 (18 dc, 6 ch-1 sps).

Rnd 2: Ch 1, sc in first st, *[ch 1, skip next st, sc in next st, ch 2, (dc, ch 2, dc) in next ch sp, ch 2], sc in next st; repeat from * 4 more times; repeat between [ ], join with sl st in first sc, fasten off (12 sc, 12 dc, 18 ch-2 sps, 6 ch-1 sps).

Rnd 3: Join white with sc in any ch-2 sp between 2 dc, ch 2, sc in same sp *[ch 2, skip next ch sp, dc in next ch sp, ch 2, skip next ch sp], (sc, ch 2, sc) in next ch sp; repeat from * 4 more times; repeat between [ ], join (18 ch-2 sps, 12 sc, 6 dc).

Rnd 4: Ch 1, sc in first st, *[sc in next ch sp, ch 1, skip next ch sp, (tr, ch 1, tr, ch 1, tr, ch 2, tr, ch 1, tr, ch 1, tr) in next dc, ch 1, skip next ch sp, sc in next ch sp, sc in next st, 2 sc in next ch sp, sc in next st, 2 sc in next ch sp], sc in next st; repeat from *; repeat between [ ], join (27 sc, 18 tr, 18 ch-1 sps, 3 ch-2 sps).

Rnd 5: Ch 1, sc in each st and in each ch-1 sp around with (sc, ch 2, sc) in each corner ch-2 sp, join (69 sc).

Rnd 6: Ch 1, sc in each st around with 3 sc in each corner ch-2 sp, join, fasten off (78).

Rnd 7: Working this rnd in **back lps** only, join black with sc in 3rd sc of any 3-sc group, sc in next 24 sts, ch 5, skip next st, (sc in next 25 sts, ch 5, skip next st) around, join, fasten off (25 sc on each edge between ch-5 sps).

Leaving ch-5 sps unworked, with black, sew **back lps** of each Triangle together according to Assembly Diagram on page 150.

INSIDE FILLER MOTIF

Rnd 1: With red, ch 6, sl st in first ch to form ring, ch 1, 12 sc in ring, join with sl st in first sc, fasten off.

Rnd 2: Join white with sc in any st, ch 2; working in sps between Triangles, sc in ch-5 sp of any Triangle, ch 2, skip next st on Motif, (sc in next st, ch 2, sc in ch-5 sp of any Triangle, ch 2, skip next st on Motif) around, join with sl st in first sc, fasten off.

Repeat Inside Filler Motif in each opening between joined Triangles.

OUTSIDE FILLER MOTIF

Rnd 1: Repeat same rnd of Inside Filler Motif.

Rnd 2: Join white with sc in any st on rnd 1, (ch 5, skip next st, sc in next st) 2 times, working on outside of Afghan where there are 4 unworked ch-5 sps, ch 2, sc in ch-5 sp on first Triangle, ch 2, skip next st on Motif, (sc in next st, ch 2, sc in ch-5 sp on next Triangle, ch 2, skip next st on Motif) 3 times, join with sl st in first sc, fasten off.

Repeat Outside Filler Motif on each area where there are 4 unworked ch-5 sps according to diagram.

Continued on page 150

Jubilee

Finished Size: 50" x 61"

Materials: Worsted-weight yarn — 24 oz. blue, 12 oz. green, 9½ oz. yellow and 7 oz. red; tapestry needle; H crochet hook or size needed to obtain gauge.

Gauge: 7 dc sts = 2"; 1 dc back lp row and 1 sc back lp row = 1".

Skill Level: ◇◇ Average

STRIP A (make 3)
First Motif

Note: Work each row or rnd in **back lps** unless otherwise stated.

Rnd 1: With blue, ch 4, sl st in first ch to form ring, ch 1, 8 sc in ring, join with sl st in first sc, fasten off (8 sc).

Rnd 2: Join yellow with sc in first st, sc in same st, 2 sc in each st around, join, fasten off (16).

Rnd 3: Join red with sc in first st, sc in each st around, join, fasten off.

Note: For **beginning V-stitch (beg V-st),** ch 5, dc in same st.

For **V-stitch (V-st),** (dc, ch 2, dc) in next st.

Rnd 4: Join green with sl st in any st, beg V-st, sc in next st, 2 sc in next st, sc in next st, (V-st in next st, sc in next st, 2 sc in next st, sc in next st) around, join with sl st in 3rd ch of ch-5, fasten off (16 sc, 4 V-sts).

Second Motif

Rnd 1: With red, repeat same rnd of First Motif.

Rnd 2: Repeat same rnd of First Motif.

Rnd 3: With blue, repeat same rnd of First Motif.

Rnd 4: Join green with sl st in any st, beg V-st, sc in next st, 2 sc in next st, sc in next st, (V-st in next st, sc in next st, 2 sc in next st, sc in next st) 2 times; to **join to last Motif made,** dc in next st, ch 1, sl st in 2nd V-st on last Motif, ch 1, dc in same st on this Motif, sc in next st, 2 sc in next st, sc in last st, join with sl st in 3rd ch of ch-5, fasten off (16 sc, 4 V-sts).

Third Motif

Rnds 1-3: Repeat same rnds of First Motif.

Rnd 4: Repeat same rnd of Second Motif.

Repeat Second and Third Motifs alternately for a total of thirteen Motifs (see Assembly Diagram on page 148).

STRIP B (make 1)
First Motif

Rnd 1: With red, ch 4, sl st in first ch to form ring, ch 1, 8 sc in ring, join with sl st in first sc, fasten off (8 sc).

Rnd 2: Join yellow with sc in first st, sc in same st, 2 sc in each st around, join, fasten off (16).

Rnd 3: Join blue with sc in first st, sc in each st around, join, fasten off.

Rnd 4: Join green with sl st in any st, beg V-st, sc in next st, 2 sc in next st, sc in next st, (V-st in next st, sc in next st, 2 sc in next st, sc in next st) around, join with sl st in 3rd ch of ch-5, fasten off (16 sc, 4 V-sts).

Second Motif

Rnd 1: With blue, repeat same rnd of First Motif.

Rnd 2: Repeat same rnd of First Motif.

Continued on page 146

Gentle Textures

Finished Size: Finished Size
35½" x 61" not including Fringe

Materials: Worsted-weight yarn — 45 oz. grey heather
and 14 oz. burgundy/teal variegated;
G and H crochet hooks or size needed to obtain gauge.

Gauge: H hook, 7 pattern sts = 2"; 11 pattern rows = 3".

Skill Level: ✧✧✧ Challenging

PANEL A (make 2)

Notes: Use H hook unless otherwise stated.

Beginning ch-2 is used and counted as first hdc.

For **half double front post stitch (fp)** *(see fig. 14, page 158)*, yo, insert hook from right to left around post of next st on row before last, yo, draw long lp through, yo, draw through all 3 lps on hook. Skip one st on last row behind fp.

Row 1: With grey, ch 18, sc in 2nd ch from hook, sc in each ch across, turn (17 sc).

Row 2: Ch 2, hdc in each st across, turn.

Row 3: Ch 2, (fp, hdc in next st) across, turn (9 hdc, 8 fp).

Row 4: Ch 2, hdc in each st across, turn.

Row 5: Ch 2, hdc in next st, fp, (hdc in next st, fp) 6 times, hdc in each of last 2 sts, turn (10 hdc, 7 fp).

Rows 6-201: Repeat rows 2-5 consecutively.

Row 202: Ch 1, sc in each st across, fasten off.

Rnd 203: For **trim,** working around outer edge, join variegated with sc in first st, sc in each st across, *ch 2, evenly space 166 sc across ends of rows, ch 2*; working in starting ch on opposite side of row 1, sc in each ch across; repeat between **, join with sl st in first sc, fasten off.

Edging

Note: For **bullion stitch (bullion st),** yo 10 times, insert hook in next st, yo, draw through st,

and carefully draw through all 11 lps on hook.

Row 1: Working in trim on one short edge of Panel A, join variegated with sc in corner ch-2 sp, ch 3, skip next 2 sts, *[(sc, bullion st 3 times, sc) in next st, ch 3], skip next 3 sts; repeat from * 2 times; repeat between [ ], skip last 2 sts, sc in next corner ch sp, turn (12 bullion sts, 10 sc, 5 ch sps).

Row 2: Ch 2, (2 hdc, ch 1, 2 hdc) in each ch-3 sp across, hdc in last sc, turn.

Row 3: Ch 1, sc in first st, (sc, bullion st 3 times, sc) in next ch sp, *insert hook in sp between 2nd and 3rd bullion sts on row 1 and in next ch sp on last row at same time, complete as sc, (bullion st 3 times, sc) in same sp; repeat from * across, sc in top of last ch-2, fasten off.

Repeat on opposite end of Panel.

PANEL B (make 3)

Row 1: With grey, ch 18, hdc in 2nd ch from hook, hdc in each ch across, turn (17 hdc).

Row 2: For **first side of first diamond,** ch 2, hdc in next 6 sts leaving remaining sts unworked, turn (7).

Row 3: Ch 2, hdc next 2 sts tog, (fp, hdc in next st) 2 times, turn (6 sts).

Row 4: Ch 2, hdc in each st across, turn.

Row 5: Ch 2, hdc next 2 sts tog, fp, hdc in each of last 2 sts, turn (5).

Row 6: Repeat row 4.

Row 7: Ch 2, hdc in same st, (fp, hdc in

Continued on page 149

Aztec Jewels

Finished Size: 42½" x 54½"
without Fringe

Materials: Worsted-weight yarn — 30 oz. each turquoise
and black, 6 oz. yellow; tapestry needle;
I crochet hook or size needed to obtain gauge.

Gauge: 3 sc sts = 1"; 3 sc rows = 1"

Skill Level: ✧✧ Average

AFGHAN

Notes: When changing colors (*see fig. 9, page 158*), always drop all colors to same side of work. Carry dropped color across to next section of same color.

Row 1: With black, ch 128, sc in 2nd ch from hook, sc in each ch across changing colors according to row 1 of graph, work between Lines A and C, repeat between Lines B and C across, turn (127 sc).

Rows 2-18: Repeating each graph row in established pattern, ch 1, sc in each st across changing colors according to graph, turn.

Rows 19-163: Ch 1, sc in each st across changing colors according to rows 1-18 on graph consecutively, ending with row 1. At end of last row, fasten off.

BOBBLE (make 111)

Leaving 6" end, with yellow, ch 4, 5 dc in 4th ch from hook, drop lp from hook, insert hook in top of ch-3, draw dropped lp through, ch 1, fasten off leaving 6" end.

Thread first 6" end from front to back through third row on one small black diamond (see photo), thread other end through fifth row. Tie ends together in a knot at back. Pull

ends back through to front and stuff inside Bobble with blunt end of crochet hook.

FRINGE

For each **Fringe,** cut 8 strands black each 12" long. With all strands held together, fold in half, insert hook in stitch, draw fold through st, draw all loose ends through fold, tighten. Trim ends.

Fringe in every 9th stitch on short ends of afghan.❧

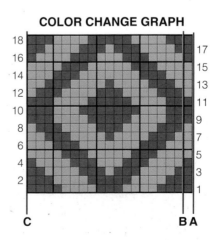

COLOR CHANGE GRAPH

Sunshine Filet

Continued from page 135

Rows 133-137: Join gold with sl st in first st, work in pattern. At end of last row, fasten off.

Rows 138-157: Join lt. yellow with sl st in first st, work in pattern, ending with row 5. At end of last row, fasten off.

EDGING

Rnd 1: Working around outer edge, in sts and in ends of rows, join lt. yellow with sc in first st, sc in same st, sc in each st and in each ch sp across with 2 sc in last st, 3 sc in first row, 2 sc in each row across; working in starting chs on opposite side of row 1, 2 sc in first ch sc in each ch across with 2 sc in last ch, 3 sc in first row, 2 sc in each row across, join with sl st in first sc, fasten off (189 sc on each short end, 315 sc on each long edge).

Rnd 2: Join gold with sc in first st, *skip next st, 5 dc in next st, skip next st, sc in next st, (skip next 2 sts, 5 dc in next st, skip next 2 sts, sc in next st) 30 times, skip next st, 5 dc in next st, skip next st, sc in next st; working across long edge, skip next st, 5 dc in next st; repeat between ( ) 52 times, skip next st*; working across short edge, sc in next st; repeat between **, join, fasten off.

Cresting Waves

Continued from page 136

EDGING

Rnd 1: Working around entire edge, in sts and in end of rows, join white with sc in ch sp of shell on bottom right corner, *ch 4, dtr in top of last sc made, (sc in next ch sp, ch 4, dtr in top of last sc made) 37 times, sc in in first row, ch 4, dtr in top of last sc made, (sc in next row, ch 4, dtr in top of last sc made) 45 times*, sc in next ch sp; repeat between **, join with sl st in first sc.

Rnd 2: Working in ch-4 sps only, sl st in first ch sp, ch 1, sc in same sp, ch 4, dtr in top of last sc made, (sc in next ch sp, ch 4, dtr in top of last sc made) around, join, fasten off.

Jubilee

Continued from page 141

Rnd 3: With red, repeat same rnd of First Motif.

Rnd 4: Join green with sl st in any st, beg V-st, sc in next st, 2 sc in next st, sc in next st, (V-st in next st, sc in next st, 2 sc in next st, sc in next st) 2 times; **to join to last Motif made,** dc in next st, ch 1, sl st in 2nd V-st, ch 1, dc in same st on this Motif, sc in next st, 2 sc in next st, sc in last st, join with sl st in 3rd ch of ch-5, fasten off (16 sc, 4 V-sts).

Third Motif
Rnds 1-3: Repeat same rnds of First Motif.
Rnd 4: Repeat same rnd of Second Motif.

Repeat Second and Third Motifs alternately, for a total of thirteen Motifs.

STRIP C (make 3)
First Half Motif
Row 1: With red, ch 2, 5 sc in 2nd ch from hook, **do not** turn, fasten off (5 sc).

Row 2: Join yellow with sc in first st, sc in same st, 2 sc in each st across, fasten off (10).

Row 3: Join blue with sc in first st, sc in same st, skip next st, sc in next 7 sts, 2 sc in last st, fasten off (11).

Rnd 4: Join green with sl st in first st, ch 5, sc in same st, sc in next 4 sts, V-st in next st, sc in next 4 sts, (sc, ch 2, dc) in last st; working in ends of rows, ch 1, sl st in side of last dc, sc in each of next 3 rows, sc in ring, sc in each of next 3 rows, sl st in 2nd ch of ch-5, sl st in 3rd ch of ch-5, fasten off.

First Full Motif

Rnds 1-3: Repeat same rnds of First Motif on Strip A.

Rnd 4: Join green with sl st in any st, beg V-st, sc in next st, 2 sc in next st, sc in next st, (V-st in next st, sc in next st, 2 sc in next st, sc in next st) 2 times; **to join to First Half Motif,** dc in next st, ch 1, sl st in V-st on First Half Motif, ch 1, dc in same st on this Motif, sc in next st, 2 sc in next st, sc in last st, join with sl st in 3rd ch of ch-5, fasten off (16 sc, 4 V-sts).

Remaining Full Motifs

Repeat Second and Third Motifs of Strip A alternately for a total of twelve Motifs and one Half Motif.

Last Half Motif

Rows 1-3: Using color sequence of blue, yellow, red, repeat same rows of First Half Motif.

Rnd 4: Join green with sl st in first st, ch 5, sc in same st, sc in next 4 sts; to join **to last Motif made,** dc in next st, ch 1, sl st in 2nd V-st on last Motif, ch 1, dc in same st on this Motif, sc in next 4 sts, (sc, ch 2, dc) in last st; working in ends of rows, ch 1, sl st in side of last dc, sc in each of next 3 rows, sc in ring, sc in each of next 3 rows, sl st in 2nd ch of ch-5, sl st in 3rd ch of ch-5, fasten off.

FIRST RIPPLE SECTION

Notes: For **single crochet decrease (sc dec),** insert hook in next ch or st, yo, draw lp through, skip next st or joining sl st, insert hook in next ch or st, yo, draw lp through, yo, draw through all 3 lps on hook.

For **double crochet decrease (dc dec),** *yo, insert hook in next st, yo, draw lp through, yo, draw through 2 lps on hook*, skip next st; repeat between **, yo, draw through all 3 lps on hook.

Row 1: Working across side of one Strip C (see diagram), with right side facing you, join blue with sc in first dc, sc in same st, skip next ch sp, (*sc in next 6 sts, sc dec, sc in next 6

sts*, sc in next ch, ch 2, sc in next ch) 12 times; repeat between **, skip next ch sp, 2 sc in last dc, turn (197 sc, 12 ch-2 sps).

Row 2: Ch 3, dc in same st, *[(ch 1, skip next st, dc in next st) 3 times, dc dec, (dc in next st, ch 1, skip next st) 3 times], dc in next ch, ch 2, dc in next ch; repeat from * 11 more times; repeat between [ ], 2 dc in last st, turn, fasten off (119 dc, 78 ch-1 sps, 12 ch-2 sps).

Row 3: Join yellow with sc in first st, sc in same st, *[(sc in next st; working behind next ch-1 sp, dc in next skipped st on row before last) 3 times, sc dec; (working behind next ch-1 sp, dc in next skipped st on row before last, sc in next st on last row) 3 times], sc in next ch, ch 2, sc in next ch; repeat from * 11 more times; repeat between [ ], 2 sc in last st, turn, fasten off.

Row 4: Join blue with sl st in first st, ch 3, dc in same st, (*dc in next 6 sts, dc dec, dc in next 6 sts*, dc in next ch, ch 2, dc in next ch) 12 times; repeat between **, 2 dc in last st, turn.

Row 5: Ch 1, 2 sc in first st, (*sc in next 6 sts, sc dec, sc in next 6 sts*, sc in next ch, ch 2, sc in next ch) 12 times; repeat between **, 2 sc in last st, turn.

Row 6: Repeat row 2.

Row 7: With red, repeat row 3.

Rows 8-10: Repeat rows 4-6.

Rows 11-21: Repeat rows 3-10 consecutively, ending with row 5. At end of last row, fasten off.

Note: When sewing pieces together, sew through **back lps** (see fig. 1, page 156) only.

With green, sew one Strip A to last row of First Ripple Section according to diagram, sew one Strip C to same Strip A.

SECOND RIPPLE SECTION

Row 1: Working across opposite side of last Strip C used (see diagram), with right side facing you, repeat row 1 of First Ripple Section.

Rows 2-21: Repeat same rows of First Ripple Section.

With green, sew one Strip A to last row of Second Ripple Section.

THIRD RIPPLE SECTION

Row 1: Working across opposite side center Strip C (see diagram), with right side facing

Continued on page 148

Jubilee

Continued from page 147

you, repeat row 1 of First Ripple Section.

Rows 2-21: Repeat same rows of First Ripple Section.

With green, sew last Strip C to Strip B.

With green, sew last row of Third Ripple Section to opposite side of Strip B.

FOURTH RIPPLE SECTION

Row 1: Working across opposite side of last Strip C (see diagram), with right side facing you, repeat row 1 of First Ripple Section.

Rows 2-21: Repeat same rows of First Ripple Section.

Sew last Strip A to last row of Fourth Ripple Section.

EDGING

Working across opposite side of Strip C on either end of afghan, with right side facing you, join blue with sl st in seam before corner, skip first ch, sc in next ch, (*sc in next 6 sts, sc in next ch, ch 2, sc in next ch, sc in next 6 sts*, sc dec) 12 times; repeat between **, sc in next ch, skip last ch, sl st in next seam, fasten off.

Repeat on opposite end of afghan.

JUBILEE ASSEMBLY DIAGRAM

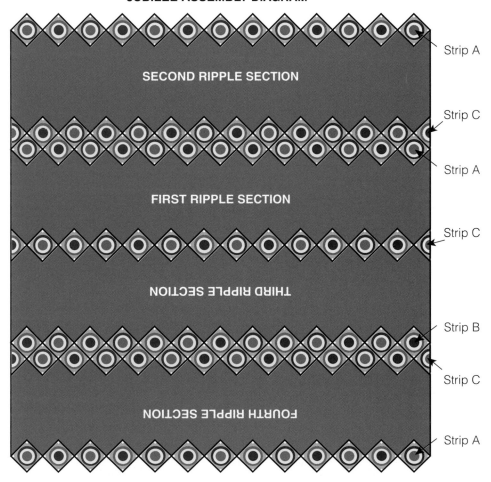

Gentle Textures

Continued from page 142

next st) 2 times, turn (6).

Row 8: Repeat row 4.

Row 9: Ch 2, hdc in same st, (fp, hdc in next st) 2 times, hdc in last st, turn (7).

Row 10: Repeat row 4, **do not** turn, fasten off.

Row 2: For **second side of first diamond,** join grey with sl st in same st as last st of row 2 on first side, ch 2, hdc in last 10 sts, turn (11 hdc).

Row 3: Ch 2, (fp, hdc in next st) across to last 2 sts, hdc last 2 sts tog, turn (10 sts).

Row 4: Ch 2, hdc in each st across, turn.

Row 5: Ch 2, hdc in next st, (fp, hdc in next st) across to last 2 sts, hdc last 2 sts tog, turn (9).

Row 6: Repeat row 4.

Row 7: Ch 2, fp, (hdc in next st, fp) across to last st, 2 hdc in last st, turn (10).

Row 8: Repeat row 4.

Row 9: Ch 2, (hdc in next st, fp) across to last st, 2 hdc in last st, turn (11).

Row 10: Repeat row 4.

Row 11: Ch 2, fp, (hdc in next st, fp) 4 times, hdc last st on this side and first st on next side tog, (fp, hdc in next st) 3 times, turn (17 sts).

Row 12: For **first side of second diamond,** ch 2, hdc in next 10 sts leaving remaining sts unworked, turn (11 hdc).

Row 13: Ch 2, hdc next 2 sts tog, (hdc in next st, fp) across to last 2 sts, hdc in each of last 2 sts, turn (10 sts).

Row 14: Ch 2, hdc in each st across, turn.

Row 15: Ch 2, hdc next 2 sts tog, hdc in next st, (fp, hdc in next st) across, turn (9).

Row 16: Repeat row 14.

Row 17: Ch 2, hdc in same st, hdc in next st, (fp, hdc in next st) across to last st, hdc in last st, turn (10).

Row 18: Repeat row 14.

Row 19: Ch 2, hdc in same st, hdc in next st, (fp, hdc in next st) across, turn (11).

Row 20: Repeat row 14, **do not** turn, fasten off.

Row 12: For **second side of second diamond,** join grey with sl st in same st as last st

on row 12 of first side, ch 2, hdc in each st across, turn (7).

Row 13: Ch 2, (hdc in next st, fp) 2 times, hdc last 2 sts tog, turn (6).

Row 14: Ch 2, hdc in each st across, turn.

Row 15: Ch 2, fp, hdc in next st, fp, hdc last 2 sts tog, turn (5).

Row 16: Repeat row 14.

Row 17: Ch 2, hdc in next st, fp, hdc in next st, 2 hdc in last st, turn (6).

Row 18: Repeat row 14.

Row 19: Ch 2, (fp in next st, hdc in next st) across to last st, 2 hdc in last st, turn (7).

Row 20: Repeat row 14.

Row 21: Ch 2, hdc in next st, (fp, hdc in next st) 2 times, hdc last st and first st on first side tog, (hdc in next st, fp) 4 times, hdc in each of last 2 sts, turn.

Rows 22-201: Repeat rows 2-21 consecutively, ending with row 21.

Row 202: Ch 1, sc in each st across, fasten off.

Row 203: For **trim,** repeat same rnd of Panel A.

Diamond Edging

Rnd 1: Working in ends of rows around one diamond opening, with G hook, join variegated with sl st in bottom point, evenly space 5 sc across to next side point, (sl st in next point, evenly space 5 sc across to next point) 3 times, join with sl st in first sl st.

Rnd 2: Ch 2; for **reverse half double crochet (reverse hdc),** working from left to right, yo, insert hook in next st to the right, yo, draw through st, complete as hdc, reverse hdc in each sc and sl st in each sl st around, join with joining sl st on last rnd, fasten off.

Edging

Work same as Panel A's Edging on page 142.

ASSEMBLY

Holding Panel A and Panel B side by side, working in sts and in ends of Edging rows, join variegated with sl st in first Edging row on

Continued on page 150

DIAMOND DREAMS   **149**   AFGHAN ENCHANTMENT

Gentle Textures

Continued from page 149

Panel A, ch 1, sc in same row, drop lp from hook, insert hook from front to back in corresponding row on Panel B, draw dropped lp through, (sc in next st or row on Panel A, drop lp from hook, insert hook in corresponding st or row on Panel B, draw dropped lp through) across, fasten off.

Join Panels together in sequence of B, A, B, A and B.

FRINGE

For **each Fringe,** cut five strands variegated each 5" long. With all strands held together, fold in half, insert hook in st or sp, draw fold through st or sp, draw all loose ends through fold, tighten. Trim ends.

Fringe in first st, last st, in each seam and in ch sps between bullion groups across Edging on one end of Afghan.✌

Rose Delight

Continued from page 139

EDGING

Rnd 1: Working around entire outer edge, join white with sc in first ch-5 sp on point of Afghan according to diagram, 2 sc in same sp, 3 sc in next ch-5 sp, [sc in each st across to next ch-5 sp, 3 sc in each of next 2 ch-5 sps, (sc in each st across to next ch-5 sp, 3 sc in next ch-5 sp, 3 dc in next ch-5 sp, 3 sc in next ch-5 sp) 4 times, (sc in each st across to next ch-5 sp, 3 sc in each of next 2 ch-5 sps) 2 times, *◊sc in each st across to next ch-5 sp, 2 sc in next ch-5 sp, 2 sc in next ch sp on Motif, 4 sc in each of next 2 ch sps, 2 sc in next ch sp, 2 sc in next ch-5 sp, sc in each st across to next ch-5 sp◊, 3 sc in each of next 2 ch-5 sps]; repeat from *; repeat between [ ]; repeat between ◊◊, join with sl st in first sc, fasten off.

Rnd 2: Join red with sl st in first st, ch 2, (sl st in next st, ch 2) around, join with sl st in first sl st, fasten off.✌

ASSEMBLY DIAGRAM

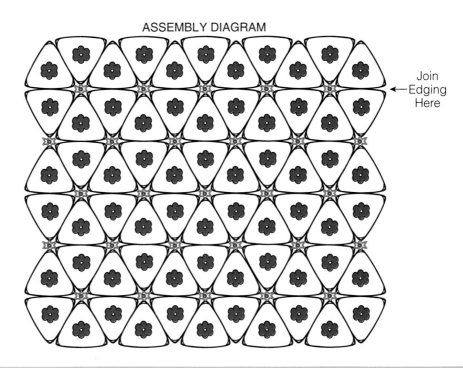

Join
Edging
Here

This book has been written in such a way that anyone, regardless of their experience, can enjoy making these patterns. Before you begin, please read the helpful information included in the next few pages to familiarize yourself with methods, terms and techniques referred to in the instructions. All basic stitches are included in the illustrated Stitch Guide. Special terms and stitches are listed in the applicable patterns.

General Instructions

Getting Started

Yarn & Hooks

When shopping for yarn, be sure to check the label for the weight specification. By using the weight of yarn specified in the pattern, you will be assured of achieving the proper gauge. It is best to purchase at least one extra skein of each color needed to allow for differences in tension and dyes.

For a neat, professional finish to your afghan, using the same brand of yarn for each color needed will enhance the looks of your work. Fiber and dye variations from one manufacturer to another can cause yarn to look and feel very different, which affects the texture and gauge of your work. If you must mix brand names to attain the colors you need, be sure to compare the yarns closely for consistency and weight, choosing the ones that are the most similar.

The hook size stated in the pattern is to be used as a guide for determining the hook size you will need. Before beginning the actual pattern, always work a swatch of an afghan's stitch pattern with the suggested hook size to check your gauge. If you find your gauge is smaller or larger than what is specified in the pattern, choose a different size hook.

Gauge

Gauge is probably the most important aspect of creating a beautiful afghan that mirrors the one in the photograph. If your gauge is too large or too small, your finished piece will probably look very different from the original.

Gauge is measured by counting the number of rows or stitches per inch. Each of the afghans featured in this book will have a gauge listed. In some patterns, gauge for small motifs or flowers is given as an overall measurement. Gauge must be attained in order for the afghan to come out the size stated, and to prevent ruffling and puckering. Usually a finished size for

blocks, motifs or strips will also be given. This will help you double-check your gauge in the end.

To check your gauge, make a swatch about 4" square in the stitch indicated in the gauge section of the instructions. Lay the swatch flat and measure the stitches over the space of several inches. If you have more stitches per inch than specified in the pattern, your gauge is too

tight and you need a larger hook. Fewer stitches per inch indicates a gauge that is too loose. In this case, choose the next smaller hook size.

Next, check the number of rows. Generally, if the stitch gauge is achieved, the row gauge will also be correct. However, due to differing crochet techniques and hook styles, you may find your stitch gauge is right, but your row gauge is not. Most crocheters with this problem achieve the stitch gauge, but find their row gauge is too short. In either case, don't change hooks, but rather adjust your row gauge by pulling the loops down a little tighter on your hook to shorten them, or by pulling the first loop up slightly to extend them.

Once you've attained the proper gauge, you're ready to start your afghan. Remember to check your gauge periodically to avoid problems when it's time to assemble the pieces, to prevent the edges of your afghan from having a wavy or V'd appearance. If you begin to notice your work getting larger or smaller, compensate by changing hooks. It is common for crocheters to "loosen up" on the gauge as they gradually become familiar with a pattern. Changing to the next size smaller hook will remedy this nicely.

Reading & Repeating

Before beginning a new pattern, read through it to familiarize yourself with the various stitches used, any notes or unusual stitches that appear or are new to you. Special instructions are typically bolded to draw your attention to them, and the stitches shown at the end of a row or round in parentheses are the stitch count for that particular row or round. Stitch counts are given so that you can check your progress on each row or round to verify its accuracy.

Written crochet instructions typically include symbols such as parentheses, asterisks and brackets used to repeat sections of the instructions. In some patterns, a fourth symbol, usually a diamond, may be added, and in rare cases a fifth symbol, typically a large dot

(known as a bullet), will be used. These symbols are signposts added to set off a portion of instructions that will be worked more than once.

Parentheses ( ) enclose instructions which are to be worked the number of times indicated after the parentheses. For example, "(2 dc in next st, skip next st) 5 times" means to follow the instructions within the parentheses a total of five times. Parentheses may also be used to enclose a group of stitches which should be worked in one space or stitch. For example, "(2 dc, ch 2, 2 dc) in next st" means to work all the stitches within the parentheses in the next stitch.

Asterisks * may be used alone or in pairs, most times in combination with parentheses. If used in pairs, a set of instructions enclosed within asterisks will be followed by instructions for repeating. These repeat instructions may appear later in the pattern or immediately after the last asterisk. For example, "*Dc in next 4 sts, (2 dc, ch 2, 2 dc) in corner sp*, dc in next 4 sts; repeat between ** 2 more times" means to work through the instructions up to

There is no need to be intimidated by lots of symbols. When followed carefully, these signposts will get you where you're going — to the end of a beautiful finished project.

For patterns with numerous repeats that can get confusing, there are several methods for marking your place for quick recognition of where you are. A few of these methods are: Mark the end of each repeat with a bobby pin; at the end of 5 or 10 repeats, remove all but the last pin. Or, keep a pad and pencil handy and make a hash-mark after completing each repeat. To tame extremely complicated patterns, write each set of instructions out on a 3" x 5" card so you can't lose your place in a long row or round.

Finishing

Patterns that require assembly will suggest a tapestry needle in the materials. This should be a #16 or #18 blunt-tipped tapestry needle. Sharp-pointed needles are not appropriate, as they can cut the yarn and weaken the stitches. When stitching pieces together, be careful to keep the seams flat so pieces do not pucker at the seams.

Hiding loose ends is never a fun task, but if done correctly may mean the difference between an afghan that looks great for years, or one that soon shows signs of wear. Always leave about 6-8" when beginning or ending. Thread the loose end into your tapestry needle and carefully weave the end through the back of several stitches. Then, to assure a secure hold, weave in the opposite direction, going through different strands. Gently pull the end, and clip, allowing the end to pull up under the stitches.

If your afghan needs blocking, a light steam pressing works well. Lay your afghan on a large table or on the floor, shaping and smoothing by hand as much as possible. Adjust your steam iron to the permanent press setting, then hold slightly above the stitches, allowing the steam to penetrate the yarn. Do not rest the iron on the afghan. Allow to dry completely.

Most afghans do not require professional blocking, but if this is your preference, choose a cleaning service that specializes in needlework. Request blocking only if you do not want the afghan dry cleaned, and attach fringe or tassels after blocking.

the word "repeat," then repeat only the instructions that are enclosed within the asterisks twice.

If used alone, an asterisk marks the beginning of instructions which are to be repeated. For example, "Ch 2, dc in same st, ch 2, *dc in next st, (ch 2, skip next 2 sts, dc in next st) 5 times; repeat from * across" means to work from the beginning, then repeat only the instructions after the *, working all the way across the row. Instructions for repeating may also specify a number of times to repeat, followed by further instructions. In this instance, work through the instructions one time, then repeat the number of times stated, then follow the remainder of the instructions.

Brackets [ ] and diamonds ◊ are used in the same manner as asterisks. Follow the specific instructions given when repeating. Sometimes, all four repeat symbols will appear in the same row or round. Simply follow the instructions as they are written, letting the symbols lead you.

Fringe

Many of the designs featured in this book require fringe, so here are a few tips for the best-looking fringe possible.

To make cutting large numbers of strands for fringe easier, use a piece of cardboard half the length of the strand needed and about 6-8" wide. Wrap the yarn around the cardboard, moving across the width, being careful not to stretch the yarn. To assure an even length, try not to layer too many wraps on top of each other. After you have finished wrapping, cut the strands at one edge of the cardboard, and you're ready to begin fringing.

Make sure the yarn for the fringe is straight before cutting. If you are using the inside of a skein and the yarn is crinkled, wrap it around the cardboard, then steam lightly to remove wrinkles and allow to dry. Re-wrap if necessary.

Trimming ends can also be a breeze if you utilize a quilter's straight edge and rotary fabric cutter. These tools are commonly available at most large fabric or variety stores and are well worth the cost if you frequently make afghans with fringe.

To use a rotary cutter, fringe the entire edge of the afghan, but do not trim the ends. Now, lay the afghan on a flat, sturdy surface over a cutting mat suitable for use with rotary cutters. Using a large-toothed comb, gently straighten the fringe strands, then lay the straight edge over the fringe where you want to cut. Simply press the cutter into the yarn and roll along the straight edge. You will have neatly cut, perfectly even fringe that looks great.

For More Information

Sometimes even the most experienced needle-crafters can find themselves having trouble following instructions. If you have difficulty completing your project, write to:

Afghan Enchantment Editors
The Needlecraft Shop
23 Old Pecan Road, Big Sandy, Texas 75755

Stitch Guide

BASIC STITCHES

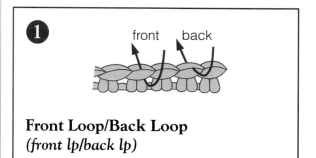

Front Loop/Back Loop
(front lp/back lp)

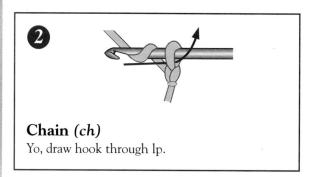

Chain *(ch)*
Yo, draw hook through lp.

STANDARD STITCH ABBREVIATIONS

The following stitch abbreviations are used throughout this book.

ch(s) . . . . chain(s)
dc . . . . double crochet
dtr . . . . double treble crochet
hdc . . . . half double crochet
lp(s) . . . . loop(s)
rnd(s) . . . . round(s)
sc . . . . single crochet
sl st . . . . slip stitch
sp(s) . . . . space(s)
st(s) . . . . stitch(es)
tog . . . . together
tr . . . . treble crochet
tr tr . . . . triple treble crochet
yo . . . . yarn over

Slip Stitch *(sl st)*
Insert hook in st, yo, draw
through st and lp on hook.

Single Crochet *(sc)*
Insert hook in st (a), yo, draw lp through, yo, draw through both
lps on hook (b).

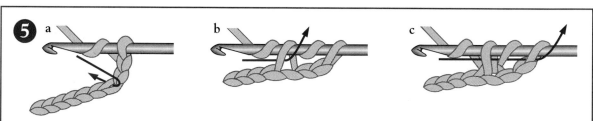

Half Double Crochet *(hdc)*
Yo, insert hook in st (a), yo, draw lp through (b), yo, draw through all 3 lps on hook (c).

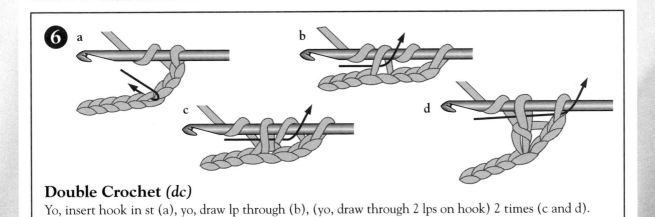

Double Crochet (*dc*)

Yo, insert hook in st (a), yo, draw lp through (b), (yo, draw through 2 lps on hook) 2 times (c and d).

Treble Crochet (*tr*)

Yo 2 times, insert hook in st (a), yo, draw lp through (b), (yo, draw through 2 lps on hook) 3 times (c, d and e).

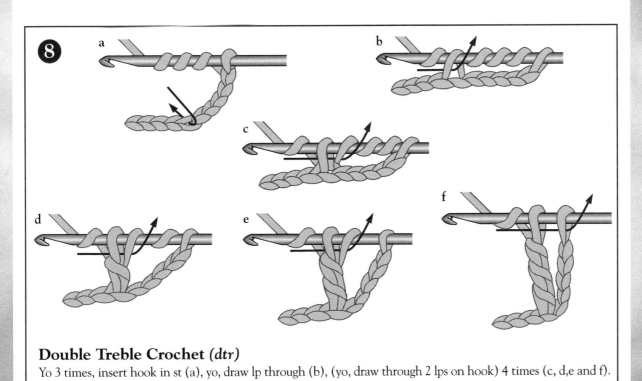

Double Treble Crochet (*dtr*)

Yo 3 times, insert hook in st (a), yo, draw lp through (b), (yo, draw through 2 lps on hook) 4 times (c, d,e and f).

CHANGING COLORS

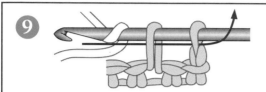

Single Crochet Color Change
(sc color change)
Drop first color; yo with 2nd color, draw through last 2 lps of st.

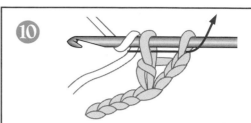

Double Crochet Color Change
(dc color change)
Drop first color; yo with 2nd color, draw through last 2 lps of st.

DECREASING

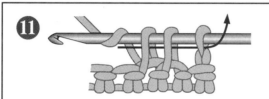

Single Crochet next 2 stitches
together (sc next 2 sts tog)
Draw up lp in each of next 2 sts, yo, draw through all 3 lps on hook.

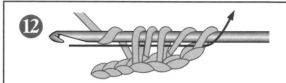

Half Double Crochet next 2 stitches
together (hdc next 2 sts tog)
(Yo, insert hook in next st, yo, draw lp through) 2 times, yo, draw through all 5 lps on hook.

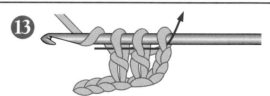

Double Crochet next 2 stitches
together (dc next 2 sts tog)
(Yo, insert hook in next st, yo, draw lp through, yo, draw through 2 lps on hook) 2 times, yo, draw through all 3 lps on hook.

SPECIAL STITCHES

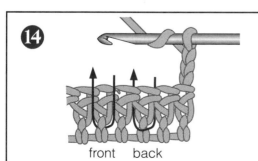

front   back

Front Post/Back Post Stitches (fp/bp)
Yo, insert hook from front to back (a) or back to front (b) around post of st on indicated row; complete as stated in pattern.

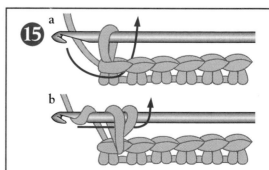

Reverse Single Crochet (reverse sc)
Working from left to right, insert hook in next st to the right (a), yo, draw through st, complete as sc (b).

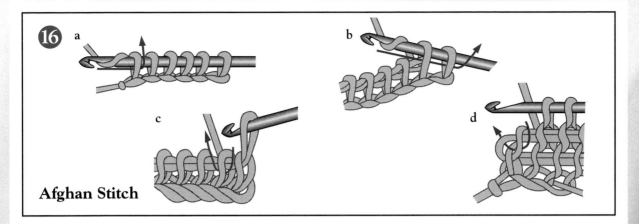

Afghan Stitch

Acknowledgments

Our sincerest thanks and appreciation goes to the following manufacturers for generously providing their product for use in the following projects:

COATS & CLARK

Country Spice . . . . *Red Heart Super Saver*
Cresting Waves . . . . *Red Heart Super Saver*
Desert Reflections . . . . *Red Heart Classic*
Ebb & Flow . . . . *Red Heart Classic*
Falling Leaves . . . . *Red Heart Classic*
Jeweltone Treasure . . . . *Red Heart Classic*
Lilac Moments . . . . *Red Heart Super Saver*
Lily of the Nile . . . . *Red Heart Super Saver*
Lover's Lace . . . . *Red Heart Classic*
Mardi Gras . . . . *Red Heart Classic*
Peaches 'n Cream . . . . *Red Heart Classic*
Remembrance Rose . . . . *Red Heart Classic*
Ribbon Candy . . . . *Red Heart Super Saver*
Shimmering Dewdrops . . . . . . *Red Heart Classic*
    & Red Heart Baby Sport
Terrace Dreams . . . . *Red Heart Super Saver*

SPINRITE

Burgundy Lilies . . . . *Bernat Berella "4"*
Calico Patchwork . . . . *Bouquet Softee*
Country Fair . . . . *Bernat Embassy*
    & Bouquet Softee Sport
Gentle Textures . . . . *Bernat Berella "4"*
    & Bernat Platinum
Medallions . . . . *Bernat Berella "4"*
Miraculous Blessings . . . . *Bernat Embassy*
Peppermint Swirls . . . . *Bernat Berella "4"*
Petit Fours . . . . *Bernat Nice 'n Soft*

CARON INTERNATIONAL

Love in Bloom . . . . *Aunt Lydia's Worsted*
Rosebuds . . . . *Wintuk*
Sunshine Filet . . . . *Wintuk*
Vintage Grapes . . . . *Wintuk*

BRUNSWICK

Floral Infatuation . . . . *Windrush*
Morning Glory . . . . *Windrush*

LION BRAND

Sentimental Journey . . . . *Jiffy Mohair*
    & Jiffy Chunky

Stitching Artists
Susie Spier Maxfield . . . . *Mardi Gras*
June Spier Batey . . . . *Irresistible Charm*
    Medallions

Photography locations and special help:

The photographs for *Afghan Enchantment* were taken at many beautiful locations in the East Texas area, including: Tankersley Gardens in Mt. Pleasant; Tyler Rose Garden in Tyler; Joan and Frank Abbott's home in Longview; Odell and Nancy Clevenger's home in Union Grove; and Rudy Beloney's home in Big Sandy. The cover photograph was taken at Tyler Rose Garden.

Special thanks to Georgia's Garden Center in White Oak and Hidalgo Imports in Longview for sharing their beautiful plants and exotic imports.

Index

Goo
rest

Goo
su